A PICTORIAL HISTORY OF
THE SEA WAR
1939–1945

A PICTORIAL HISTORY OF
THE SEA WAR
1939–1945

Paul Kemp

NAVAL INSTITUTE PRESS
Annapolis, Maryland

CONTENTS

First published in the UK by Arms & Armour Press, an imprint of Cassell plc, London

Published and distributed in the United States and Canada by The Naval Institute Press 118 Maryland Avenue Annapolis, Maryland 21402-5035

Library of Congress Catalog Card No. 95-71396

ISBN 1-55750-674-4

This edition is authorized for sale only in the United States, its territories and possessions, and Canada

Edited by Michael Boxall

Designed by Roger Chesneau/DAG Publications Ltd

Printed and bound in Great Britain

INTRODUCTION

Title page photograph: USS *Oklahoma* capsized alongside USS *Maryland* following the Japanese attack on Pearl Harbor, Sunday 7 December 1941.

This spread: A sloop pitches heavily as she manoeuvres in convoy KMF.1 in October 1942. KMF.1 was an assault convoy sailing direct from the Clyde to North Africa. Virtually the entire British First Army was carried by this convoy and landed on the shores of North Africa in Operation 'Torch'. Together with American convoys which sailed direct from the USA, this was the first major Allied amphibious operation of the war.

For an author to be asked to condense the war at sea during the Second World War into approximately four hundred and fifty photographs is to be asked to squeeze a gallon into the proverbial pint pot. The choice has not been easy and when one photograph has been selected, often another three or four equally worthy photographs have had to be discarded. For those who fail to find the ship or campaign in which they participated within these pages, I can only apologise. The photographs have been selected from a number of archives throughout the world and I am deeply grateful to the staffs of those institutions and my various 'sleuthers', who have helped to find many of the illustrations.

From 3 September 1939 until 2 September 1945 war raged in every ocean of the world. It is obviously impossible to provide a comprehensive coverage of every theatre or engagement but it is hoped that the photographs in this book will give some idea of the nature of naval war from 1939 to 1945.

1. FLEET ACTIONS

During the First World War the British Grand Fleet faced the German High Seas fleet across the North Sea and this stand-off was the dominant feature of the war at sea until the German surrender in 1918. During the Second World War there was no such stand-off and as a result surface operations were far more flexible. Although the German fleet was numerically small, forces had to be maintained in home waters to guard against a breakout into the Atlantic or an attack on a Russian convoy.

In the Mediterranean the large Italian fleet was dominated by the British throughout the war. Early

Below: A British battle squadron on exercises before the Second World War. Behind the battleships, cruisers of the *Southampton* class deploy to form a reconnaissance screen.
Right: The same sort of thing in the United States Navy: battleships engage in intricate manoeuvres. Planners in all navies still thought in terms of the single decisive engagement between opposing battle fleets.

actions at Calabria and Spartivento showed that the Italians were not prepared to come to grips with the Royal Navy and British ascendancy was confirmed by the victory at Matapan in April 1941.

In the Pacific and Indian Ocean the huge distances involved meant that aircraft carriers became the dominant weapon and capital ships were 'relegated' to shore bombardment tasks or providing fast AA guardships for the carriers. The battleship's swansong came during the Battle of Leyte Gulf when six veteran American vessels destroyed two Japanese in what was the last battleship-versus-battleship engagement of the war.

Below: In reality things were to be very different. The German pocket battleship *Admiral Graf Spee* enjoyed a brief career as a commerce raider in the South Atlantic, sinking nine ships, during the autumn and winter of 1939. On 13 December 1939 she was brought to action off the River Plate by the cruisers *Exeter*, *Ajax* and *Achilles* and after a series of engagements throughout the day (in which *Exeter* was badly damaged and had to retire) she sought refuge in Uruguayan waters in the port of Montevideo.

Left: Damage to the *Graf Spee* sustained during the action. Note the burned-out Arado Ar 196 floatplane on the catapult. In fact, *Graf Spee*'s damage was not particularly significant.
Below: British cruisers wait outside Uruguayan territorial waters: HMS *Ajax* (in foreground) and *Cumberland*. The British first tried to persuade the Uruguayan authorities to insist that *Graf Spee* leave, but then decided to keep the ship blocked in Montevideo until reinforcements arrived.

Right: The end finally came on 17 December when *Graf Spee*'s commanding officer, *Kapitän zur See* Hans Langsdorff, decided that he had had enough. Worn down by exhaustion and the burdens of command, he took his ship into the channel between Uruguayan and Argentine waters and had the crew taken off in a tender (shown here alongside *Graf Spee*'s starboard quarter). Shortly after 18.15 scuttling charges blew the ship apart.

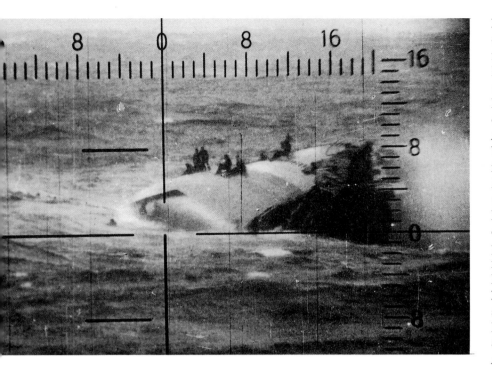

Left, upper: The Norwegian campaign was the focus for much naval activity. Here the British destroyer HMS *Glowworm* is in the final stages of her engagement with the cruiser *Admiral Hipper* on 8 April 1940. *Glowworm* had become detached from her formation and had run into *Hipper*. In a one-sided fight *Glowworm* was battered into a hulk before her commanding officer (subsequently awarded a posthumous Victoria Cross) rammed *Hipper*, tearing a huge hole in her side.

Left, lower: British destroyers steam down Ofotfjord towards Narvik on 13 April 1940 in the Second Battle of Narvik. On 10 April two British destroyers had been sunk while attacking a force of seven German destroyers at Narvik. Three days later the British returned in superior numbers, including the battleship *Warspite*.

Below: The German destroyer *Erich Giese* beached after the Second Battle of Narvik. Altogether the Germans lost eight modern destroyers and a submarine in the battle of 13 April. British casualties amounted to one damaged destroyer.

Far left, upper: The German battlecruisers *Scharnhorst* and *Gneisenau* in action against the British aircraft carrier *Glorious* on 8 June 1940. Although *Glorious* and her two attendant destroyers *Ardent* and *Acasta* were sunk with great loss of life, *Scharnhorst* was struck by a torpedo fired by the sinking *Acasta*. A few days later *Gneisenau* was torpedoed by HMS *Clyde*. Both ships were out of action for more than six months. All in all the Norwegian campaign cost the German Navy dear – three capital ships damaged and eight destroyers sunk – and these losses meant that it was in no position to implement the planned invasion of England.

Far left, lower: The Mediterranean was the focus for much naval activity. A large Italian fleet was matched by a quantitatively inferior British force but one which was dynamically led by Admiral Sir Andrew Cunningham. The engagement off Calabria on 9 July 1940 was the first between the British and Italian fleets. After a two-hour duel the Italian battleship *Guilio Cesare* was struck by a 15in shell from *Warspite* at a range of 26,000 yards. The Italians retired, which indicated their reluctance for a prolonged action.

Left, upper: The Italian cruiser *Bartolomeo Colleoni* on fire after a long chase off Crete on 19 July 1940 by HMAS *Sydney* and the destroyers *Hyperion* and *Ilex*. *Colleoni* was supposedly the 'fastest ship in the world', but this boast did her little good. A shell hit set off her forward magazines and she was eventually sunk by torpedo.

Left, lower: The most significant engagement in the Mediterranean was the Battle of Matapan on 28/29 March 1941 in which the Italians lost the cruisers *Zara*, *Fiume* and *Pola*, seen here in happier days at Naples before the war.

Above: A photograph showing the Italian cruisers under attack by Swordfish aircraft from HMS *Formidable*. The Italian fleet had sortied to attack convoys bound for Greece and after a brief engagement with Cunningham's light forces was attacked by British aircraft in an attempt to slow them down so that Cunningham's battlefleet could catch up. The battleship *Vittorio Veneto* was hit by one torpedo, as was the cruiser *Pola* which was disabled. The Italian commander then made the fateful decision that the cruisers *Zara* and *Fiume* turn back and take their stricken consort in tow.

Above: A dramatic painting showing the night action at Matapan. Cunningham disregarded conventional wisdom and pressed on into the night. The three Italian cruisers were totally unprepared for action with British capital ships and were sunk in short order together with the destroyers *Alfieri* and *Carducci*. Matapan established for the Royal Navy a moral ascendancy over the Italians which was never lost.

Left, upper: The scene shifts to the Atlantic where in May 1941 the German battleship *Bismarck*, seen here in the Baltic, sortied on a commerce raiding operation in company with the cruiser *Prinz Eugen*.

Left, lower: *Bismarck*'s departure from the Baltic was reported by British sources in Sweden and confirmed by this RAF reconnaissance photograph of Grimstadt Fjord taken on 21 May 1941 showing her at anchor. The motives of the German commander (Vice-Admiral Günther Lütjens) for the stand-off at Grimstadt Fjord are unclear – especially as he did not use the opportunity to fuel and since the stay exposed his force to detection by British reconnaissance.

Above: Once *Bismarck*'s departure was confirmed all available British forces were deployed to meet the threat. Convoy sailings were interrupted while the battlecruiser HMS *Hood*, pride of the Royal Navy and known as the 'Mighty Hood', and the battleship HMS *Prince of Wales* sailed for the Denmark Strait between Iceland and Greenland – *Bismarck*'s likely route into the Atlantic.

Left: Able Seaman Alfred Newall of the cruiser HMS *Suffolk*, on patrol with her consort *Norfolk* in the Denmark Strait, who first sighted the *Bismarck* on 23 May 1941.

Top, left: The last known photograph of HMS *Hood* taken in the evening of 23 May 1941. Early the next morning the British force encountered *Bismarck* and after a brief engagement *Hood* blew up and sank. Various theories have been advanced for her loss, the most likely being that a 15in shell hit from *Bismarck* caused a cordite fire in a 4in HA magazine which blew out a bulkhead leading to massive structural failure.

Top, right: A dramatic photograph taken from *Prinz Eugen* showing *Bismarck*'s 'Caesar' and 'Dora' turrets ('X' and 'Y' turrets in British parlance) firing on *Hood*. From *Hood*'s ship's company of more than 1,400 there were but three survivors.

Above: A distant view of the engagement taken from *Prinz Eugen*. On the right smoke rises from the wreck of HMS *Hood* while on the left *Prince of Wales* retires under a smokescreen. The decision of *Prince of Wales*'s commanding officer to break off the action was morally courageous: his ship was new, not worked up and damaged.

Below: *Bismarck* (seen here after the action with *Hood*) did not get away without damage. A 14in shell from *Prince of Wales* struck forward and caused a severe loss of fuel. Lütjens was forced to abandon his operation and head for a French port and repairs. Thereafter his ship was continually attacked – by aircraft from *Victorious* on the night of 24/25 May, by aircraft from *Ark Royal* on 26 May and by destroyers on the night of 26/27 May.

Bottom: The end came on the morning of 27 May when *Bismarck* was engaged by the battleships *King George V* and *Rodney* of the Home Fleet. In a two and a half hour gun duel *Bismarck* was battered into a hulk. This photograph shows a 16in salvo from *Rodney* falling around *Bismarck*.

Above: A lightly retouched (for the benefit of the Press) photograph showing *Bismarck* sinking after being scuttled by a torpedo fired by the cruiser *Dorsetshire*. It has always been a matter of contention as to whether *Bismarck* was sunk or was scuttled. In the event it is of little consequence: given the amount of damage she had sustained and the rising sea state, her end was inevitable.

Below, left: Survivors from *Bismarck* wait to be picked up by HMS *Dorsetshire*. Only 115 were saved of a ship's company of more than 2,000.

Below, right: HMS *Prince of Wales* sinking on 10 December 1941 after being attacked by Japanese aircraft off the coast of Malaya. Lacking air cover, *Prince of Wales* and her consort *Repulse* were easy game for the well-trained Japanese aircrew. The sinking of the two British capital ships in such a short time showed just how vulnerable such ships were to air attack unless they had their own organic air cover.

Above: HMS *Exeter* sinking during the Battle of the Java Sea on 27 February 1942. This battle was a courageous but futile attempt by a heterogeneous British, Australian, Dutch and American force to stop the Japanese invasion of Java.

Right: Two photographs showing damage to the destroyer *Worcester* sustained during the 'Channel Dash' – the breakout of *Scharnhorst* and *Gneisenau* from the French port of Brest up the English Channel to Germany. After an unsuccessful air attack off Dover the German ships were engaged by destroyers off Harwich, again without effect. Although both ships were damaged by mines, they reached Germany safely. The Channel Dash was a propaganda *coup*, but it was a pyrrhic victory for the Germans as both ships were now removed from the Atlantic theatre.

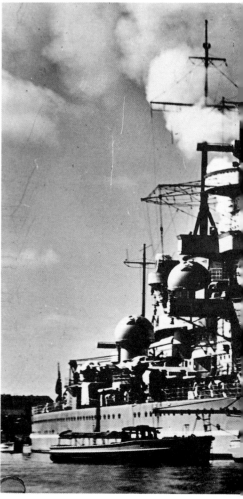

Top: The German battleship *Tirpitz*, which moved to Norway in the spring of 1942. From then until her loss in November 1944, *Tirpitz* influenced British planning to a considerable extent. The mere fact that she was thought to be at sea was responsible for the decision to order Convoy PQ.17 to scatter in July 1942.

Above: The single occasion on which *Tirpitz* fired her guns in anger was during a bombardment of Barentzburg on Spitzbergen on 2 September 1943.

Left: The battlecruiser *Scharn-horst* whose luck finally ran out on 26 December 1943 when she was sunk during the Battle of the North Cape. While attempting to attack convoy JW.55B *Scharnhorst* was driven off by the cruiser screen and event-ually retired. On her way back to Altenfjord she was inter-cepted by the battleship *Duke of York* and sunk by gunfire and torpedo. Only thirty-six of her complement of 1,836 survived. *Scharnhorst*'s sinking in effect marked the end of operations by German capital ships outside the Baltic.

Above: The year 1943 ended with another decisive victory for the Royal Navy, this time in the Bay of Biscay. On 28 December 1943 the cruisers *Glasgow* and *Enterprise* sank the German destroyer *Z27* and the escorts *T25* and *T26* (out of a force of eleven ships deployed) during a German operation to bring home a blockade runner. Here *Glasgow*, seen from *Enterprise*, forges ahead.

Above: Although there were few major fleet actions in home waters, there was no shortage of work for capital ships. Shore bombardment was one such operation – here *Warspite*, veteran of Narvik, Matapan and Salerno, bombards 'Gold' Beach during the 1944 Normandy landings.

Right: One aspect of ship-versus-ship engagements which went on throughout the Second World War was the war between motor torpedo boats of all countries. Here Vosper-type British MTBs are seen secured at their base in Felixstowe.

Bottom, far left: Survivors from a German *Schnellboot* sunk in the North Sea are landed by HMS *Garth* at Harwich on 18 February 1943. Duels between MTBs were fast and furious.

Bottom, centre: A German *Schnellboot* captured in the North Sea but which sank while being towed back to port.

Right, top: A camouflaged Italian MTAS boat in the Mediterranean. The Italians were particularly successful with this type of craft, sinking the cruiser *Manchester* in August 1942.

Right, centre: A splendid aerial view of an American PT boat in the Pacific.

Right, bottom: The wreck of the German destroyer *Z32* beached at the Isle de Baz near Barfleur after being driven ashore by the Canadian destroyers *Haida* and *Huron*.

Left, top: The Japanese battleship *Yamashiro* under air attack during the Battle of Leyte Gulf, 23–26 October 1944. Leyte Gulf was a three-pronged Japanese assault on the beachhead established by the Americans at Leyte in the Philippines. It was a classic Japanese plan devised to confuse, break up and destroy the American naval forces before rolling up the invasion shipping.

Left, centre: The Japanese battleship *Musashi* under attack on 24 October. Armed with nine 18.1in guns, she was sunk by up to nineteen air-dropped torpedoes and seventeen bombs.

Left, bottom: Events reached a climax on 25 October when Admiral Kurita's force penetrated the San Bernadino Strait unchallenged and met a weak force of American escort carriers and destroyers off the east coast of Samar Island. For three hours the Americans bravely held the Japanese off, though the escort carrier *Gambier Bay* was lost and three destroyers were sunk. This photograph shows the *Gambier Bay* under attack and sinking.

Right, upper: On the night of 25 October the American battleships delivered their revenge for Pearl Harbor. Six old battlewagons had been formed into a task group under the command of Rear-Admiral Jesse Ohlendorf. In the Surigao Strait they ambushed the Japanese battleships *Fuso* and *Yamashiro* and sank them. The cruiser *Mogami* was crippled and only the destroyer *Shigure* escaped. In this photograph the fires in the distance are the *Yamashiro* and *Mogami* burning. Leyte Gulf was one of the great naval battles of the Second World War. The Japanese lost three battleships, four carriers, ten cruisers and nine destroyers and the battle marked the virtual end of the Imperial Japanese Navy as a fighting force.

Right, lower: An aerial photograph showing the pocket battleship *Lützow* lying at Swinemünde on 16 April 1945. The ship's stern is on the bottom after being damaged in an air raid by RAF aircraft using the 12,000lb Tallboy bomb. Note the huge crater carved out of the bank by a near miss. The capital ship, which had dominated naval warfare for centuries, had been eclipsed by air power.

2. CARRIER WAR

The Second World War saw the aircraft carrier emerge as the most potent striking weapon in the war at sea. At the end of the First World War Britain had led the way in naval aviation with a large force of land-based aircraft and thirteen seaplane carriers in commission. The Royal Navy used aircraft extensively for ASW purposes and were contemplating a surprise air attack on the German High Seas Fleet at its Wilhelmshaven anchorage when the war ended. The shape of things to come was clearly visible for those with eyes to see.

During the inter-war period, however, naval aviation languished. Budgets were tight and navies were dominated by gunnery officers who regarded the battleship as the final arbiter of naval warfare. Nevertheless, enough work had been done to ensure

Below: HMS *Ark Royal*, Britain's newest aircraft carrier at the outbreak of the Second World War, with one of her Swordfish circling overhead. She was the first large, purpose-built aircraft carrier to be commissioned by the Royal Navy and could embark sixty aircraft.

Above: HMS *Courageous* sinking on 17 September 1939 after being torpedoed by *U29*. *Courageous* was engaged in anti-submarine operations when she was sunk, and her loss prompted the British to abandon the policy of using large fleet carriers for ASW. She was one of a class of three 'large light cruisers' built during the Great War which were all converted to aircraft carriers. Of her two sisters, *Glorious* and *Furious*, only *Furious* would survive the war.

that when war broke out again in 1939 each of the major navies had some sort of naval air arm.

In practical terms naval aviation was the preserve of Britain, Japan and the United States. Germany and Italy dabbled in this aspect of warfare, but their plans were frustrated and the carriers produced by the Germans and Italians languished at their moorings.

Britain showed the way with the carrier strike on Taranto in November 1940 when a force of antiquated Swordfish altered the balance of power in the Mediterranean overnight. Thirteen months later the Japanese did the same at Pearl Harbor. But it was the Americans who became masters of the art of carrier warfare. The nature of the campaign in the Pacific necessitated the build-up of strike forces composed of carriers and fast battleships which could range far afield of land bases and hit Japanese ships and bases at will. These carrier task forces, supported by organic logistic elements, became formidable instruments of power. Moreover the industrial might of America meant that carrier and aircraft losses could easily be sustained. The Japanese surrender may have been signed on the deck of a battleship, but it was the aircraft carrier which was the real victor.

Above: TSR (Torpedo Strike Reconnaissance) Swordfish aircraft ranged on *Ark Royal*'s flight deck in pre-war exercises. The antiquated looking Swordfish was Britain's newest carrier aircraft in 1939 and despite appearances gave yeoman service in all roles including, on one occasion, as a night-fighter.

Below, left: The harbour at Taranto in Italy photographed on 10 November 1940 by an RAF Maryland flying from Malta. The Italian fleet was numerically superior to the Royal Navy and exercised considerable influence on British operations in the Mediterranean. Admiral Sir Andrew Cunningham resolved to mount a carrier strike at Taranto to reduce the threat.

Above: HMS *Illustrious*, the carrier employed by Cunningham in the operation at Taranto. *Illustrious* had only been

completed in May 1940 and had been sent straight out to the Mediterranean. The attack was launched on the night of 11 November using 21 Swordfish aircraft flown off in two waves. The operation was a complete success and, despite AA fire, only two aircraft were lost.

Left: The morning after: the battleship *Conte di Cavour* beached and leaking oil after being struck by one torpedo which tore a 60 square foot hole in the hull. Although she was repaired the ship did not see service again.
Above: The battleship *Littorio* down by the bows after the attack. Total Italian casualties at Taranto were three of six battleships damaged (one permanently) and two heavy cruisers damaged. Overnight the balance of power had been altered in Britain's favour: the awesome striking power of carrier aviation had been demonstrated for the first time.

Left: May 1941 saw the German battleship *Bismarck* sortie into the Atlantic on a commerce raiding operation. Virtually the entire Royal Navy in home waters was mobilised to hunt the *Bismarck* down, including the carriers *Victorious* with the Home Fleet and *Ark Royal* operating with Force H out of Gibraltar. Here Swordfish are ranged on *Victorious*' flight deck before the strike launched on 24 May. One hit was scored but it did little or no damage to the German battleship.

Left: The erratic wake left by *Bismarck* after *Ark Royal*'s aircraft attacked on 26 May. After a mistake in which the cruiser *Sheffield* was attacked, the aircraft were flown off again and scored three hits. Two were insignificant, but the third disabled the ship's steering and effectively sealed her fate.

Below, left: HMS *Ark Royal* sinking on 13 November 1941 after completing a ferrying operation to Malta. *Ark Royal* seemed to bear a charmed life: on several previous occasions the Germans had claimed that she had been sunk. Her luck ran out when she was torpedoed by *U81*. Valiant efforts to save her failed and she rolled over and sank next day.

Below: *Ark Royal* survivors at Gibraltar. Only one man of her complement of 1,580 was lost.

Right, top: HMS *Victorious* in northern waters in early 1942. The decision to send supplies to the north Russian ports of Murmansk and Archangel meant that a carrier had to be kept in northern waters to provide a strike capability against the German battleship *Tirpitz* based in Norway.

Far right, upper: An Albacore aircraft taking off from HMS *Victorious*. On 9 March 1942 Albacores from 817 Squadron embarked in *Victorious* made an unsuccessful torpedo attack on *Tirpitz*. The attack was pressed home with almost suicidal bravery but no hits were scored.

Right, centre: HMS *Indomitable* escorting the August 1942 convoy to Malta, Operation 'Pedestal'. 'Pedestal' was the largest carrier operation mounted in European waters by the Royal Navy: three fleet carriers were directly employed (*Eagle*, *Indomitable* and *Victorious*) with two carriers (*Argus* and *Furious*) in support.

Right, bottom: HMS *Eagle* sinking on 11 August 1942 after being torpedoed by *U73*. *Eagle* was the last of the five British fleet carriers that were sunk during the Second World War.

Far right, lower: One of the best-known photographs of the Second World War: a view from the island of HMS *Indomitable* showing *Victorious* leading *Eagle* in the early stages of Operation 'Pedestal'.

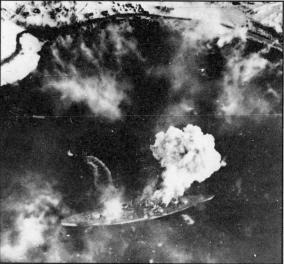

Main illustration: HMS *Furious*, doyenne of British naval aviation. After the 'Pedestal' convoy British fleet carrier operations concentrated in northern waters where in the summer of 1944 a concerted carrier offensive was mounted against the German battleship *Tirpitz*. *Furious* took part in many of these operations, despite her age (she was launched in 1916). At one stage in the summer of 1943 she was the only operational carrier available to the Home Fleet.

Above, left: Operation 'Tungsten', a carrier attack on *Tirpitz* at Kaafjord in April 1944. *Tirpitz* was attacked by Barracudas flying from the carriers *Furious*,

Formidable and *Indefatigable*; some of the aircraft had been modified to carry a 1,600lb bomb. Here pilots prepare for the operation aboard *Furious*.

Above, centre: Some hits were scored on *Tirpitz*, seen here on fire during the attack, and she was badly damaged. But she was not sunk, so the carrier attacks continued throughout the summer.

Above, right: Handlers rush to secure a Barracuda returning after the 'Tungsten' strike.

Above: The escort carrier HMS *Nairana* in the Clyde on completion in February 1944. Escort carriers were built using merchant ship hulls and machinery or converted from merchant ships already under construction (*Nairana* was built as the *Port Victor* until purchased). Fleet carriers took too long to build in any number so escort carriers, or 'Woolworth carriers' as they were known, filled the gap – and did so very creditably.

Right: HMS *Avenger*, an American-built escort carrier, under way with her 'air group' of six Sea Hurricanes ranged on deck. Two Swordfish aircraft were also carried in the hangar. *Avenger* proved the worth of this type of vessel during the passage of Convoy PQ.18 to the USSR in September 1942 when her fighters successfully broke up massed torpedo-bomber attacks.

Right, top: An Avenger from an escort carrier flying over a convoy. Convoy protection was the main role of escort carriers in home waters, although at times they might be required for fleet operations.

Right, centre: Escort carriers operated in all kinds of weather. This is the flight deck of HMS *Fencer* returning from Russia in April 1944. In such conditions the pilots in the open cockpits of the Swordfish aircraft were frozen stiff and on more than one occasion had to be lifted out of the cockpit after an operation.

Right, bottom: HMS *Nairana* seen from the flight deck of HMS *Campania* during the passage of convoy RA.64 from the USSR in February 1945. Flying operations took place in all but the foulest weather.

Top, left: Towards the end of the war, with the U-boat threat diminishing, escort carriers were used on more offensive operations. Here aircraft from HMS *Searcher* and *Trumpeter* attack German shipping near Narvik on 4 May 1945 – the Fleet Air Arm's last operation in home waters.

Above: The MAC (Merchant Aircraft Carrier) was another ingenious solution to the shortage of carriers. Bulk grain carriers or tankers had their superstructures removed and replaced by a flight deck – this is *Empire MacAlpine*. The ships were an unusual but successful marriage of merchant ship and carrier and there was a good *esprit de corps* among their mixed mercantile and naval crews. Some aircraft even had the 'Royal Navy' legend replaced by 'Merchant Navy'.

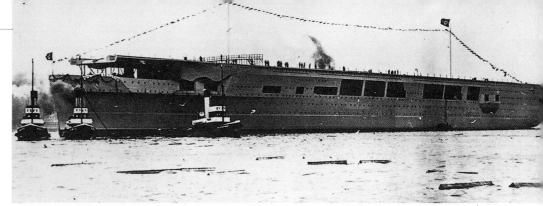

Left, upper: Lieutenant-Commander Ransford Slater makes the first deck landing on *Empire MacAlpine*, 7 May 1943. The aircraft is just about to engage the arrester wire. Only nineteen merchant ships were converted to MAC ships – the conversion was long and expensive, and escort carriers were being built more quickly and more cheaply in America.

Left, lower: The flight deck of *Empire MacAlpine* showing four Swordfish ranged. Note the very small size of the flight deck. Each MAC ship could carry four aircraft. Some had hangars – in those that did not the aircraft had to be kept on deck in all weathers.

Top: The launch of the German aircraft carrier *Graf Zeppelin* on 8 December 1938. *Graf Zeppelin* was the first such ship built by the Germans and was to carry a mixed complement of Bf 109 and Ju 87 aircraft modified for naval service. However, this was as far as Germany's naval aviation programme got. The ship's construction was repeatedly abandoned and re-started and she was eventually scuttled at Stettin.

Above: Italy's carrier programme fared no better. This is the *Aquila*, abandoned at Genoa in 1945. *Aquila* had been converted from the liner *Roma* but her construction was interrupted by the Italian armistice of 1943 when she was sabotaged to prevent her take-over by the Germans. She was then further damaged in an air raid and in an attack by British Chariots before being scuttled at Genoa.

Left, top: The Japanese aircraft carrier *Akagi*. Like many of the carriers which made up the backbone of the inter-war fleets, *Akagi* and her sister ship *Kaga* were converted from the hulls of capital ships abandoned under the terms of the Washington Naval Treaty of 1922. *Akagi* was to be the flagship for the greatest surprise carrier strike in history – the Japanese attack on Pearl Harbor.

Left, centre: 'Battleship Row' at Pearl Harbor in the early moments of the attack. By the summer of 1941 the Japanese felt that only military action would solve the various diplomatic and economic problems facing their country. Given America's superiority, the Japanese resolved to strike first, and did so early in the morning of Sunday 7 December 1941 using a force of six carriers. The American fleet was caught in a low state of readiness. The controversy rumbles on to this day as to exactly who in the US command was responsible.

Left, bottom: Battleship Row after the attack. *Arizona*, *California*, *West Virginia* and *Oklahoma* were sunk: *Maryland*, *Nevada*, *Tennessee* and *Pennsylvania* were damaged. Three cruisers, three destroyers, a seaplane tender and a repair ship were also damaged, while a minelayer and a target ship were sunk. A total of 2,334 US personnel perished, including Vice-Admiral Isaac C. Kidd who was killed aboard the *Arizona* while manning a machine gun. He was the highest ranking US naval officer to be killed in the war. Fortunately the American carriers were at sea and missed the attack. They were to exact a terrible revenge on the Japanese.

Left: The explosion of the forward magazine of the destroyer USS *Shaw* in dry dock.
Below: The destroyer *Shaw* in the floating dock after the explosion of her magazine. The front section of the ship was destroyed as far back as the bridge.

Right: The end of the battleship *Arizona*: nearly half the US casualties at Pearl Harbor were sustained when the ship exploded. Today *Arizona* is a memorial to those killed in the attack.

Below: USS *Nevada* beached at Hospital Point after her unsuccessful attempt to reach the open sea.

Right: USS *Pennsylvania*, the fleet flagship, in dry dock. In the foreground are two wrecked destroyers, *Cassin* and *Downes*. *Cassin* had been hit and had rolled over on to *Downes*.
Below: Salvage operations on the *California*. The American battleships sunk or damaged at Pearl Harbor, with the exception of *Arizona* and *Oklahoma*, were salvaged and recommissioned after refit and they played an important role in the subsequent defeat of Japan.

Left, top: After Pearl Harbor the Japanese carriers turned west into the Indian Ocean where their aircraft sank the old British carrier *Hermes* on 9 April 1942.

Left, centre: The American response to Pearl Harbor: a B-25 bomber takes off from the USS *Hornet* to attack Tokyo in the famous 'Doolittle Raid' on 18 April 1942. Sixteen aircraft took part, and although the damage inflicted on Japan was slight, the psychological impact of the raid was immense.

Left, bottom: Another view of a B-25 labouring into the air. Two of the aircraft crashed in Japanese-occupied China and one landed in the USSR and was interned. The other thirteen all reached Nationalist China and safety.

Left, top: The Battle of the Coral Sea, 6–8 May 1942, during the Japanese advance on New Guinea and Australia, was the first of many Pacific battles which were conducted entirely by carrier aircraft – the fleets did not come into contact. Here the Japanese carrier *Shokaku* turns under attack on 8 May.

Left, centre: The end of the USS *Lexington*, sunk in a counter-attack by seventy Japanese aircraft. Great efforts were made to save her but she went down on the evening of 8 May after a series of internal explosions. Although the Americans lost more *matériel* in the battle, they won the strategic advantage.

Left, bottom: The Japanese carrier *Akagi* circling and on fire during the Battle of Midway, 4–6 June 1942. This battle marked a turning point in the Pacific war: the Japanese lost four carriers (*Akagi*, *Kaga*, *Hiryu* and *Soryu*) with more than 200 aircraft and their experienced crews. It was a defeat from which Japanese naval aviation never recovered.

Above: The Americans did not escape loss-free at Midway. Aircraft from *Hiryu* found the American carrier *Yorktown* and damaged her; two days later she was finished off by the Japanese submarine *I168*.

Right, upper: One of the first major operations for the American carrier task groups was a raid on the harbour of Rabaul in New Guinea, where a powerful Japanese squadron threatened US forces engaged at Bougainville. A surprise strike was planned using the carriers *Saratoga* and *Princeton*. Here grim-faced pilots walk out to their aircraft.

Right, lower: Flight deck crew 'hit the deck' during an attack on a US carrier engaged in softening-up operations on the island of Kwajalein in the Marshalls in December 1943.

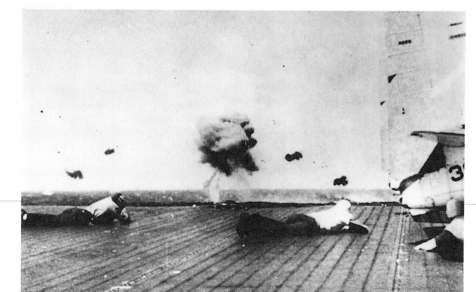

Above: The F4U Corsair, a carrier-based fighter which was initially rejected by the US Navy for carrier service. Corsairs saw extensive service with the British Fleet Air Arm, although the aircraft's real reputation was won in the ground attack role with US Marine Corps squadrons.

Right, upper: F6F Hellcat aircraft ranged on the deck of a carrier prior to take-off. The Hellcat was the first carrier fighter which could engage the Japanese A6M Zero on equal terms and is credited with 4,947 of the 6,477 Japanese aircraft destroyed in the air during the Second World War.

Right, lower: A pilot makes a quick exit from his F6F Hellcat during operations on board the USS *Cowpens* in 1944.

Above: A TBM Avenger flying over an atoll in the Marshall Islands in early 1944 after the islands had been taken. The Avenger was the US Navy's principal carrier-borne torpedo bomber from 1942. It first saw action at Midway and thereafter served continuously. Avengers operating from carriers of TF.58 were responsible for sinking the Japanese battleship *Yamato* on 7 April 1945.

Below: The SB2C Helldiver, which replaced the Dauntless but which never achieved the popularity of its predecessor. Production was delayed, and although the prototype flew in December 1940 the first aircraft did not go to sea until November 1943.

Bottom: Smoke rises from burning Japanese shipping at Truk in the Caroline Islands. In February 1944 a carrier task force consisting of nine carriers under Admiral Marc Mitscher struck at the island in a series of raids in which over 45,000 tons of Japanese shipping was sunk, together with 168 aircraft destroyed – all for the loss of six US aircraft.

Above: The SBD Dauntless was the most effective dive-bomber of the Second World War in terms of warship tonnage sunk. SBDs were responsible for the sinking of four Japanese carriers at the Battle of Midway on 4 June 1942. Though nominally replaced by the SB2C Helldiver, the SBD continued to serve in a wide variety of roles until the end of the war.

Left: An excellent photograph showing an SBD about to be waved off from the flight deck.

Above, left: A torpedo strikes home on a Japanese transport at Truk on 16 February 1944.

Above, centre: USS *Shangri-La* going down the ways at Norfolk Navy Yard on 24 February 1944. *Shangri-La* was one of the famous Essex-class carriers – 'Champions of the Pacific' – which formed the backbone of American carrier task forces.

Each displaced more than 34,000 tons at full load and could carry more than 90 aircraft.

Below: An American carrier task force of the Third Fleet at anchor in the Marshall Islands in the Pacific. The carrier task groups, made up of carriers and fast battleships, were the most potent aspect of American naval

power in the Pacific and spearheaded the twin amphibious campaigns of the central and south-west Pacific fronts. Nine carriers and twelve battleships are visible in this picture together with a large number of cruisers, destroyers and other ships.

Top, right: The 'Ready Room', where pilots rested between operations and where they were briefed about objectives.
Above: A carrier task group at sea. In the foreground is an *Independence* class light carrier built on the hull of a *Cleveland* class cruiser; in the background is an *Essex* class carrier. Behind are a number of battleships whose role in fast carrier operations was the provision of massed defensive AA fire.

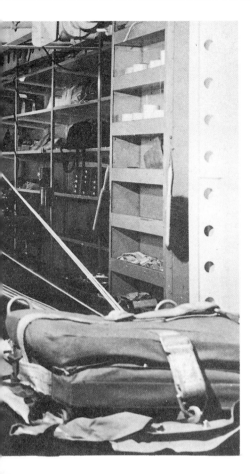

Above, far left: American personnel apply rising sun stencils to the door of their crew room aboard a carrier. Each stencil represents a Japanese aircraft shot down.

Above, centre: Parachute packing aboard the USS *Bennington*.

Above, right: An unusual use for one of the lift wells on the flight deck of an American carrier.

Far left: The air plot aboard the USS *Bennington*, where the movements of aircraft within radar range of the ship were monitored.

Left: Hellcat fighters struck down in *Bennington*'s hangar. The photograph was taken during the ship's shakedown cruise – normally the hangar would be a crowded and busy space.

Above: A dynamic photograph showing the Landing Signal Officer aboard the USS *Yorktown* signalling to a pilot to cut his throttle and land. The 'talker' in the foreground relays information from the bridge and flying control in the island.

Right, top: Japanese aircraft carriers at sea before the Battle of the Philippine Sea on 19/20 June 1944. The American invasion of the Marianas prompted the Japanese to begin a series of massive carrier-based and land-based air strikes on the American carrier task forces in the Philippine Sea. Nine Japanese carriers were employed in the operation.

Left, centre: A Nakajima B5N torpedo-bomber begins its take-off run, 19 June 1944. The Japanese forces were simply decimated: more than 300 of their aircraft were shot down in what the Americans called 'The Great Marianas Turkey Shoot'. Moreover, the carriers *Taiho* and *Shokaku* were sunk by American submarines and *Hiyo* was sunk by American aircraft the next day.

Left, bottom: The censor appropriately captioned this photograph 'a deck load of disaster for the Japanese': a mixed group of Hellcats, Avengers and Helldivers ranged on the flight deck.

Right, top: The first carrier in the Fast Carrier Task Force to be sunk was *Princeton*, bombed on 24 October 1944 during the Battle of the Philippine Sea. Here the carrier manoeuvres astern of a battleship earlier that day while a pall of black smoke marks the spot where a Japanese aircraft has crashed on being shot down.

Right, centre: The USS *Intrepid*'s crew battle to repair a damaged flight deck after the ship was bombed on 25 October 1944 off Luzon in the Philippines. As the war neared the Japanese home islands the US carriers became the focus for attacks by Japanese suicide bombers, the *Kamikaze*s. The ships' wooden flight decks made them extremely vulnerable to this form of attack. However, the Americans' immense superiority in numbers of ships and aircraft meant that losses could easily be made good.

Right, bottom: Smoke rises from the USS *Saratoga* after a Japanese attack off Iwo Jima, 21 February 1945.

Above, left: The forward end of *Saratoga*'s flight deck, showing two Hellcat aircraft and the remains of a third. *Saratoga* was struck by four bombs and two *Kamikaze*s while providing air support for the Marines ashore.

Below: The USS *Franklin* on fire after being struck by a Japanese *Kamikaze* during operations off Okinawa on 19 March 1945. A total of 832 personnel died in or after the attack and only damage control of a high order saved the ship. As the American advance neared Japan the carriers were called upon to act as floating airfields in support of amphibious operations – and in so doing they became exposed to Japanese suicide attacks and suffered accordingly.

Above, centre: The USS *Bunker Hill* on fire on 11 May after being hit by two *Kamikaze*s which penetrated the carrier's layered defences.
Above, right: The British carrier task force at Ulithi in the Pacific in April 1945. From top to bottom: HMS *Victorious*, *Illustrious*, *Unicorn*, *Indefatigable* and *Indomitable* – the apotheosis of British naval aviation in the Second World War.
Below: Nothing demonstrated the supremacy of the carrier more than the Battle of the East China Sea on 7 April 1945 when aircraft from TF.58 reached out and sank the Japanese behemoth *Yamato*.

3. THE DEFENCE OF SEABORNE TRADE

All belligerents depended, to a greater or lesser extent, upon the free movement of their merchant shipping either in direct support of military operations or for the import/export of raw materials essential to the war effort. The country which depended most upon its merchant shipping was Great Britain. Britain was, and is, a manufacturing nation unable to feed itself and dependent on the import of food and raw materials for survival. This was not a new problem for the British, who since the thirteenth century had used the convoy system, in which the movement of merchant shipping was organised and given protection by the state, as the best means of sustaining and protecting their maritime trade in time of war. The system served Britain well and apart from a brief and disastrous departure during the First World War, it remained the linchpin of British maritime strategy. Convoy is both a defensive and offensive modus operandi: merchant ships are

Left: Munitions, in this case high explosives, arriving at a British port from Canada during the Second World War. Every conceivable commodity came across to Britain by sea, brought by the 'unsung heroes' of the Merchant Navy.

Above: An aerial view of a convoy at sea. A convoy could number as many as fifty vessels spread over fifty square miles of ocean. All ships were required to sail in convoy except for those with a speed greater than fifteen knots. It was felt, correctly, that these ships possessed sufficient speed to outrun a U-boat in all but the most unfavourable circumstances.

given protection and the aggressors, be they submarines or surface raiders, are denied the initiative.

During the Second World War Britain used the convoy system both to protect her maritime trade and to deploy the forces necessary to pursue the war in overseas theatres such as the Middle East and the Pacific. There were two sorts of convoys: commerce and operational. Commerce convoys were those bringing the raw materials and food necessary to keep Britain's economy going and her people fed. Operational convoys were those in support of a specific political or military objective. These included convoys carrying supplies to North Russia after Britain's decision to aid that country following the German invasion in June 1941, convoys to support the beleaguered garrison at Malta and troop convoys carrying men and equipment to all parts of the world.

Undoubtedly the Atlantic route was the most critical for Britain. This was the route along which most of Britain's food and raw materials came, and across which the thousands of American troops came to launch the various invasions in North Africa, Italy and eventually, Normandy. The Battle of the Atlantic was the longest of the war, lasting from the sinking of the *Athenia* on 3 September 1939 to the sinking of U881 by an American destroyer less than 48 hours before the capitulation of Germany in May 1945. The battle reached its most critical point in the late spring and early summer of 1943 when German U-boats almost succeeded in severing the North Atlantic seaway.

Above, left: Before the sailing of a convoy there would be a meeting of the Masters of the merchant ships, the Commanding Officers of the escorts, the Convoy Commodore and the relevant officers from the shore staff. The route to be taken and signalling arrangements would be discussed and grievances would be aired. It was traditional for ships' Masters to wear civilian clothes at such conferences.

Above: Checking a life raft on a merchant vessel before sailing. Such rafts were placed on slides over the ship's side so they could easily be dropped into the water if required. They carried minimal supplies of food and water, but to be cast adrift in one was a bleak prospect.

In terms of operational convoys the most important routes were those to North Russia and Malta. Both these routes passed through areas where there were strong concentrations of enemy forces, and the North Russia route had the added disadvantage of weather conditions which bordered on the limits of human endurance. The operation of these convoys was governed by political and strategic necessities rather than military ones and accordingly losses were high: in the Halberd Malta convoy of June 1942, 50 per cent of the ships were sunk en route and only one reached Malta undamaged.

In other theatres the convoy system was equally important. Although the United States showed some initial reluctance to adopt convoy, and thereby lost a considerable amount of shipping as a result, it eventually did so in both the Atlantic and Pacific where the supply lines stretched from America's west coast to, eventually, the shores of Japan. In Europe merchant shipping was less important to the Axis powers since most cargoes could be carried by land. In the Mediterranean, however, the Axis relied on shipping to support their armies in North Africa. These convoys proved acutely vulnerable to attack as a consequence of the restricted area in which they operated (there is little choice of route between Naples and Tripoli whereas a British trade convoy had the

Far left: A convoy seen from the bridge of a destroyer. In the early days of the war, before the development of refuelling facilities, the escorts could only go part of the way before having to turn back to fuel.

Left: An East Coast convoy assembles under the protective umbrella of barrage balloons at a British port. Even this route was vulnerable to attack by German aircraft and, especially, fast motor torpedo boats or *Schnellboote*.

entire Atlantic in which to manoeuvre), and the Allied success in breaking Axis codes meant that their shipping could be located with almost uncanny precision. The interdiction of the Axis trans-Mediterranean supply route was of major significance in causing the collapse of German/Italian forces in North Africa.

In the Far East Japan was in a position similar to that of Britain. Japan was an industrial nation with hardly any natural resources to sustain her people and industry. It was the lack of indigenous raw materials that caused Japan to embark on an expansionist policy in China and South East Asia which eventually led to war with America and Britain. It is therefore simply staggering that once war had been declared Japan made no effort at all to defend its maritime trade. The attention of the Japanese Navy was firmly fixed on the titanic battle with the Americans which they felt would decide the war's outcome, and it was not until January 1944 that Japan adopted a convoy system and by then it was too late. Most her merchant shipping had been sunk by American submarines or fallen victim to air-laid mines. Japan's failure to protect her maritime trade meant that, effectively, she was starved into surrender before either of the atomic bombs was dropped.

Right: A convoy seen from a Sunderland flying boat of RAF Coastal Command. In the early stages of the war air cover could only be provided in coastal waters. This photograph was taken early in the war as many of the ships are still wearing peacetime liveries – in time these would be replaced by the ubiquitous and more practical grey overall scheme.

Left, upper: A tanker in heavy North Atlantic weather. Not only did the convoys have to contend with the U-boat menace but there was the constant battle with the sea. Under these conditions life aboard ship could easily degenerate into an endless misery of continual watches, cold food, little sleep and constantly wet clothes.
Left, lower: A convoy passes through the Straits of Dover. Channel convoys ran the risk of bombardment from heavy German guns in the Pas de Calais in addition to the usual threats from submarines, *Schnellboote* and aircraft.

Right: The Convoy Commodore, a retired naval officer, sometimes of great seniority and distinction brought out of retirement, whose role was to direct the movements of the convoy as a whole. He was not in charge of the escorts: they were under the Senior Officer (who was usually very junior to the Commodore), but naturally no escort commander would lightly ignore a suggestion from the Commodore. The Commodores were a splendid body of men who endured the rigours of life in the North Atlantic with an equanimity worthy of men half their age.

Top: Officers on the bridge of an escort watch the merchant ships in their charge. Relations between the Royal Navy and the Merchant Navy were not always smooth. The sturdy independence manifested by the Merchant Navy throughout the war in the face of operational command by the Royal Navy often brought the latter to despair. Nevertheless, shared privations of the war at sea engendered a mutual respect.

Above: Heading homewards, the British destroyer HMS *Vanoc* passes an outward-bound coastal convoy in March 1941. The convoy system was like a spider's web covering the world and providing the basis for Allied victory.

Left: A merchant ship loaded with the 'stuff of war' heads eastwards across the Atlantic. Her holds are crammed with munitions and vehicles and on the hatches are stowed three Lockheed Hudson aircraft.

Below: A 'Flower' class corvette in mid-Atlantic. This class, based on a commercial whale-catcher design, will for ever be associated with the Battle of the Atlantic and has been immortalised in Nicholas Montserrat's novel *The Cruel Sea*.

Above, far left: A quiet, almost peaceful, interlude aboard the Polish vessel *Warsarwa* en route for Greece in May 1941. Conditions were not always as tranquil as seen here.

Above: The perils of sailing independently: the liner *Doric Star* is finished off by a torpedo from the pocket battleship *Admiral Graf Spee* on 2 December 1939. She was sailing alone because the convoy system was not fully operational at this time. Convoy was the best defence against attack and on only one occasion was a convoy scattered by a surface raider.

Left: Troops crowd the rails of the liner *Stirling Castle* at Liverpool before their departure for the Middle East. Troop convoys, known as 'WS' or 'Winston Specials', ran regularly from the UK to the Middle and Far East throughout the war. They were composed of large liners and were heavily escorted. Each of their voyages was practically a major fleet operation.

Above, right: Troops parade aboard the liner *Empress of Australia* while on passage in August 1941. The WS convoys were faster than the norm and since they had the freedom of the oceans to manoeuvre in,

they suffered little interference from the enemy.

Below: The pocket battleship *Admiral Scheer* in raiding guise with a false bow wave. On 5 November 1941 *Scheer* attacked convoy HX.84 (37 ships). The armed merchant cruiser *Jervis Bay* was sunk while giving the convoy time to disperse and as a result 32 ships escaped. After this incident convoys were given capital ships as escorts and this was sufficient to deter a surface raider. *Scharnhorst* and *Gneisenau* backed away from convoy SL.67 on 8 March 1941 when the ancient battleship *Malaya* was sighted.

Right: No convoy was immune from attack, however. This is the liner *Viceroy of India* sinking on 11 November 1942 after being torpedoed by *U407* off Algiers. The 'Torch' landings had prompted a massive concentration of German and Italian submarines in waters around Gibraltar and the North African littoral.

Below: The merchant ship *Orari* in Grand Harbour Malta in June 1942 after the arrival of two ships out of six in the Harpoon convoy. Malta was an important base for British ships, submarines and aircraft engaged in operations against Axis shipping in the Mediterranean. The British were determined to keep Malta and thus were prepared to accept the large losses incurred on Malta convoys between the summer of 1940 and November 1942. But by summer 1942 the island's supplies were low and the spectre of surrender loomed unless another convoy could be fought through.

Above, far right: As a desperate measure the fast minelayer HMS *Welshman* made three round trips to Malta carrying important supplies. *Welshman* had a top speed in excess of 37 knots and was considered fast enough to proceed independently. Here she is shown arriving on 15 June 1942 on her second trip disguised as a Vichy French *Leopard* class destroyer. Hours later, her cargo discharged, *Welshman* headed back to sea.

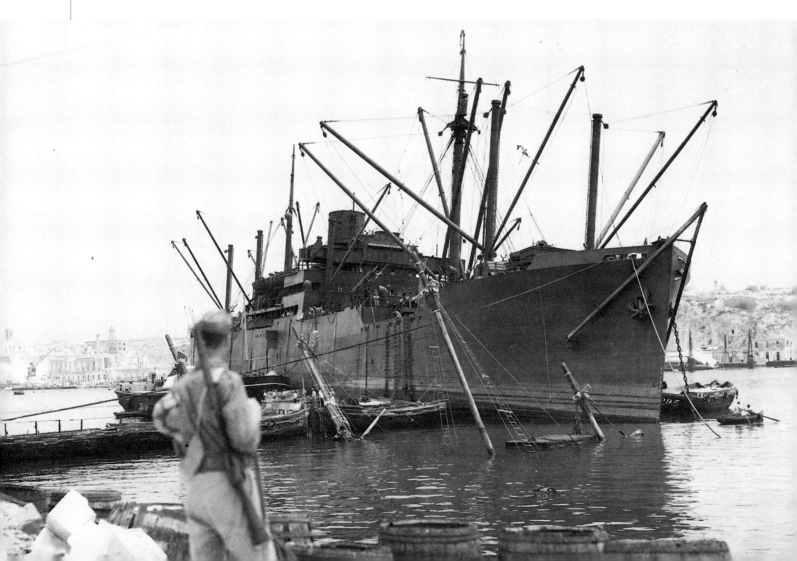

Left, upper: Throughout the siege of Malta, submarines played a vital role in carrying supplies to the island – the famous 'Magic Carpet' service. Here members of the crew of the minelaying submarine HMS *Porpoise* show off their 'Jolly Roger' commemorating nine such trips to Malta. The letters 'PCS' stand for Porpoise Carrier Service.

Left, lower: Hideous confusion in the mine deck aboard *Manxman* (a sister ship to *Welshman*) during a supply trip to Malta in November 1942. Munitions, food, dried milk and military personnel are all piled in together. These extempore operations were useful in their way, but to survive Malta needed supplies on a scale that could only be brought in by a convoy.

Right: An Italian photograph showing the 'Pedestal' convoy to Malta under attack in August 1942. Consisting of thirteen merchant ships and a tanker, 'Pedestal' was escorted by no fewer than two battleships, four carriers, seven cruisers and twenty-six destroyers. Their struggle to get through was one of the epics of the war: nine of the merchant ships were sunk, together with an aircraft carrier, two cruisers and a destroyer, but enough supplies reached Malta to enable the island to carry on.

Below: Of all the ships in the 'Pedestal' convoy, the most important was the tanker *Ohio*. She was torpedoed on 12 August by the Italian submarine *Axum* and was further damaged in subsequent air attacks. Determination and magnificent seamanship by her crew and the naval escorts ensured her arrival in Grand Harbour to a tumultuous welcome on 15 August.

Far left, bottom: The route to North Russia was another area where convoys operated in the teeth of enemy opposition to support a strategic objective – in this case keeping the USSR in the war. From July 1941 to May 1945 a total of 41 convoys sailed for the Soviet ports of Murmansk and Archangel. These convoys became notorious because of the atrocious weather which bordered on the limits of human endurance. This photograph shows convoy JW.53 ploughing through thin pancake ice in February 1943.

Below, centre: A cloud of smoke marks the spot where the Soviet tanker *Azerbaijan* was hit during the passage of convoy PQ.17 in July 1942. PQ.17 was run in midsummer against the advice of the Admiralty. It attracted its fair share of air and submarine attacks but was stoutly defended. In this case, after a pause to recover themselves, *Azerbaijan*'s crew got their ship under way again and eventually reached port.

Above, right: The German surface battle group assembled in Altenfjord, waiting for the order to sortie against PQ.17. Viewed from *Tirpitz* are the cruiser *Hipper* (right) and pocket battleship *Lützow* (left). The move of the ships from Trondheim had been detected by the RAF but not their subsequent arrival at Alta. Taking counsel of his fears and ignoring intelligence indicators which placed the German ships in port, Admiral Sir Dudley Pound, who was controlling the operation from London, ordered the convoy to be scattered. Twenty-four of the thirty-seven merchant ships were sunk.

Below: The classic Arctic convoy photograph showing PQ.18 under air attack in September 1942. Although almost half the ships were lost, it was fought through to Russia with great gallantry and represented a significant victory.

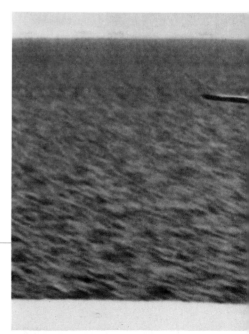

Far left, upper: A merchant-man labouring in heavy seas during the passage of convoy RA.64 from the USSR to the UK in February 1945. Foul weather was not unusual in the Arctic, but the storm which struck this convoy was such that no fewer than twelve of the escorting destroyers needed docking for structural damage.

Far left, lower: German troops disembarking in North Africa. The Axis had to supply their armies by sea, using the comparatively short route from southern Italian ports to Benghazi or Tripoli. But this route lay within easy striking distance for British forces based in Malta.

Left, top: HMS *Aurora* leads Force K into Grand Harbour on 10 November 1941 after sinking an entire Italian convoy. British forces based on the island took a heavy toll of Axis vessels and thus exercised an important influence on the course of the Desert War. Lack of petrol (because most of his tankers had been sunk) stopped Rommel at Alam Halfa and denied him freedom of movement at El Alamein.

Left, centre: A transport flying the German ensign survives a near miss from a Beaufighter based in Malta.

Left, bottom: The requirement to sink as much Axis shipping as possible meant that every aircraft that could fly was brought into service. Here a Wellington, better known for high-level bomber operations, delivers a low-level torpedo attack on an Axis convoy.

Above: In home waters the Germans used shipping for some movements but it was never as vital to them as it was to the Allies. A German convoy is seen here off the Norwegian coast in July 1944: three of the ships were sunk and the rest damaged. Attacks were pressed home by the Beaufighters at masthead height.

4. SUBMARINE WAR

The fact that submarine operations, in particular the sinking of merchant shipping without warning, is prohibited by International Law, was disregarded by all the belligerents during the 1939–45 war. Germany, Italy and America ignored it from the outset while Britain gradually adopted unrestricted warfare over a period of time.

Germany and the USA used their considerable submarine fleets to wage commerce war. The German U-boats came within a whisker of victory in the spring of 1943 before superior anti-submarine measures told against them. Although the introduction of new, sophisticated submarines such as the Type XXI and Type XXIII promised much, they came too late to have any significant effect on operations. In the Pacific American submariners succeeded in starving Japan into surrender by waging a ferocious campaign against shipping. Between these two campaigns the British waged a small but not insignificant submarine campaign against Axis supply lines in the Mediterranean.

Far left, bottom: The sinking of the liner *Athenia* on 4 September 1939 marked the beginning of Germany's campaign against British shipping in the Atlantic. HMS *Fame* stands by to rescue survivors.

Left, upper: Shocked *Athenia* survivors are taken ashore in Ireland.

Left, lower: A U-boat at sea in heavy weather. At the outbreak of the war Germany had but thirty-six U-boats available for commerce raiding.

Above: A U-boat commander at the periscope, in this case *Kapitänleutnant* Adalbert Schnee of *U201*. In the early days of the war U-boat commanders did little shooting while dived, preferring instead to engage on the surface at night to make use of their boats' greater speed and manoeuvrability.

Below: The bridge of *U552* at sea, with the lookouts scanning their allotted sections of the horizon. Before the advent of long-range air patrols U-boats were virtually immune from attack in the central Atlantic and could spend the day on the surface to recharge their batteries before using the cover of darkness for convoy attacks.

Left, upper: *U564*, a typical Type VIIC U-boat, sets off from a French port for an Atlantic patrol in November 1941. Throughout the war the Type VIIC formed the bulk of Germany's submarine force and remained virtually unaltered. The Germans' occupation of the French Atlantic ports meant that their submarines no longer had to make the long and dangerous trip around the north of Scotland or through the Dover Straits to get to their hunting-grounds in the Atlantic.

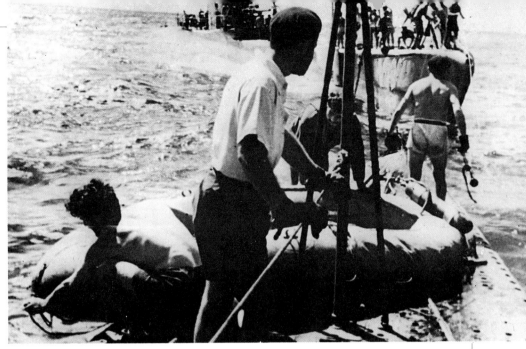

Left, lower: A merchant ship pays the price for trying to make an independent passage. *U123* sinks her in a leisurely daylight action in early 1942.

Above, left: HMS *Barham* explodes after being torpedoed by *U331* in the Mediterranean on 25 November 1941. Less than five minutes after the torpedo struck *Barham* blew up with the loss of 862 of her crew.

Below, left: In the early days of the war success was the norm for U-boat crews. Convoys were lightly escorted, if at all, and the British had not yet built up

much experience in ASW. Here *Kapitänleutnant* Schultz of *U48* receives news of his Knight's Cross while at sea and is solemnly awarded an *Ersatz* version produced by his engine room department.

Above, right: To make the most of their U-boat's sea time the German command evolved a means of supplying them in mid ocean using either tankers or specially constructed supply submarines, the Type XIV 'milch-cows'. U-boats could be supplied with everything from torpedoes to fuel, though fresh

food was obviously out of the question. Here two U-boats rendezvous in mid ocean and are using a light jackstay transfer to move supplies.

Below, right: The crew of *U124* looking relaxed at a mid ocean rendezvous in May 1941. Such replenishment operations ceased after the introduction of mid Atlantic air patrols and the breaking of German naval codes.

Above, left: Rear-Admiral Karl Dönitz and his staff discuss operations. Throughout the war Dönitz maintained a very tight control of U-boat operations, using radio to alter the disposition of his boats at sea. He never realised that successful British code-breaking operations made this control his Achilles' heel.

Right, lower: British submarines alongside a depot ship in Scottish waters. Although the British submarine fleet scored some successes in the Norwegian Campaign, its role in home waters for the rest of the war was relatively inactive. There were innumerable patrols in bad weather off the Norwegian coast in the hope that *Tirpitz* or one of her consorts would emerge. British submariners in home waters echoed the lot of their predecessors in the Great War when they complained that all they saw was 'water and a damn sight too much of that!'

Above, centre: A Type VII U-boat under air attack as a depth-charge explodes on her port side. She was *U625*, sunk by an RCAF Sunderland of No 422 Squadron west of Ireland on 10 March 1944.

Above, right: A dramatic picture showing an attack by aircraft from the escort carrier USS *Card*. One of the falling depth-charges has been circled by the censor; two of the U-boat's crew can be made out huddled by the conning tower.

Right: A Type VII dives quickly while under air attack from an RAF Sunderland. Aircraft made the passage through the Bay of Biscay while entering or leaving port especially hazardous.

Above: *U266* sinks in a welter of foam on 14 May 1943 north of the Azores, the first victim of FIDO, the air-launched acoustic homing torpedo known more formally as the Mk XXIV mine.
Left: *U505* in US hands after being captured on 4 June 1944 by sailors from USS *Pillsbury*. After a depth-charge attack she came to the surface, her commanding officer believing her damaged beyond repair. *Pillsbury*'s sailors had prepared for just such an eventuality and boarded the boat, dismantled scuttling charges and shut off flood valves. *U505* was the first vessel captured on the high seas by the US Navy since the war of 1812. She is now preserved in Chicago.

Left. upper: A Type XXI U-boat, *U2354*, under air attack on 6 May 1945 while heading for a Norwegian port. The Type XXIs possessed enhanced endurance and armament and would have been formidable had they entered the war earlier. The German failure to pursue replacements for the Type VII design meant that they were outstripped by Allied developments in ASW.

Left, lower: The Japanese destroyer *Yamakaze* sinking on 25 June 1942 after being torpedoed by the American submarine *Nautilus*.

Below: An old American S-boat arrives at Dutch Harbor, Alaska, after a patrol off the Aleutians. The S-boats were not suited to operations and their crews endured considerable privations.

Right, upper: Admiral Chester W. Nimitz, CinC Pacific Fleet, decorates Lieutenant-Commander Thomas Klakring of the USS *Guardfish* with the Navy Cross. Klakring was one of the first commanders to undertake a successful patrol in Japanese waters.

Right, lower: Lieutenant-Commander Dudley 'Mush' Morton on the bridge of USS *Wahoo* with his executive officer Lieutenant Richard O'Kane. Morton was another commander who made an early mark.

Below: USS *Tautog*, top-scoring American submarine of the Second World War. The photograph shows her in an early configuration with minimal gun armament and large conning tower.

Left: A *Fubuki* class destroyer damaged by *Wahoo* in a 'down the throat' shot at Wewak in 1943.

Below: The commanding officer of an American submarine at the search periscope in the control room. Behind him, at the large wheel, is one of the hydroplane operators. The depth gauge obligingly reveals that this photograph was taken when the boat was on the surface.

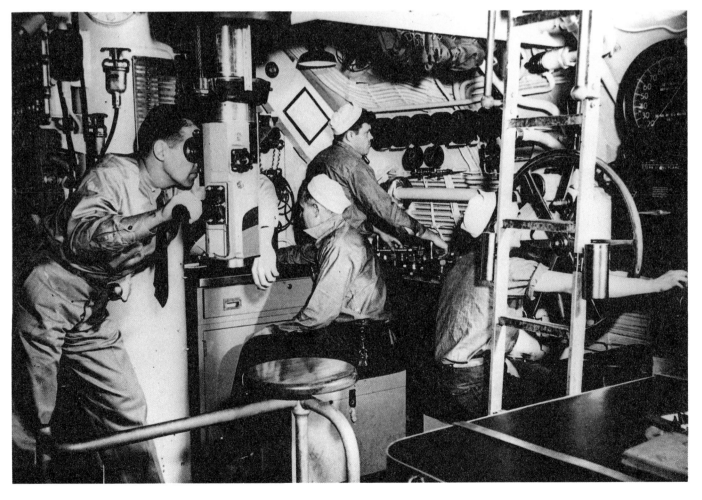

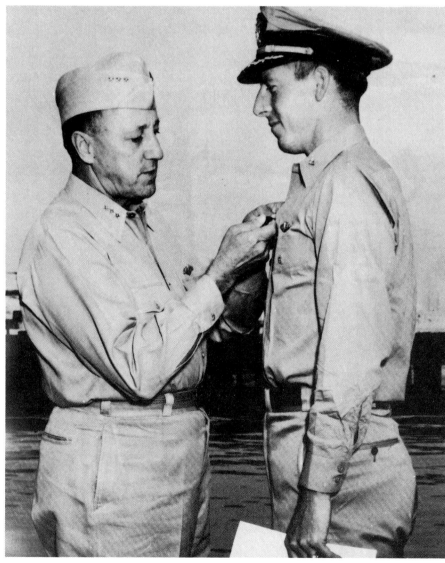

Left, upper: The Japanese liner *Ryuko Maru* being given the *coup de grâce* by the American submarine *Puffer* on 1 January 1944.

Far left, lower: Lockwood awards the Navy Cross to Commander Eugene Fluckey of USS *Barb* in August 1945. Fluckey was one of the most enterprising of Lockwood's commanders.

Below: The USS *Tang*, one of the very successful *Gato/Balao* class which made up the bulk of the American submarine fleet. She is shown as completed. The class proved capable of absorbing a good deal of modification as a result of war experience.

Bottom, centre: A much modified USS *Hawkbill* seen at the end of the war, carrying a heavy gun armament of two 5in guns, one 40mm Bofors and a 20mm Oerlikon. Submarines like *Hawkbill* virtually starved Japan into surrender by decimating her merchant fleet.

Bottom, right: The most significant success scored by British submarines in the Far East was the sinking of the Japanese cruiser *Ashigara* by HMS *Trenchant* in the Banka Strait on 8 June 1945. *Ashigara* was hit by five of the eight torpedoes fired in a technically flawless attack.

Main illustration: British U-class submarines in Malta. It was in the Mediterranean that British submariners found a real chance to strike at the enemy, attacking Axis convoys heading to and from North Africa. The 'U' class, small and handy, proved particularly suitable for this theatre of operations.

Far left: Lieutenant David Wanklyn on the bridge of his submarine *Upholder*. Despite a shaky start, Wanklyn became the most proficient of British submarine commanders until he perished on his last patrol in April 1942. When news of his death was announced the Admiralty issued an unprecedented communiqué to the effect that 'the ship and her company are gone but the example remains'.

Left: The Italian cruiser *Muzio Attendolo* at Messina after being torpedoed by HMS *Unbroken* on 13 August 1942. *Attendolo* lost the first 60 feet of her bows.

5. ANTI-SUBMARINE WARFARE

he war against submarines was of particular relevance to Britain and the USA, who depended on free passage of the oceans for supplies and troop movements. They devoted huge resources, material and technical, into beating the U-boats – and they succeeded.

Germany and Italy were bothered by Allied submarine operations, but were not threatened to the same degree. German ASW was adequate but the Italians proved very proficient, although they were aided by a very favourable environment. The Japanese should have been concerned about ASW but were not. It was not until late in the war that the IJN began to devote resources to ASW, but by then it was too late.

Below: Admiral Sir Max Horton, Commander-in-Chief Western Approaches, in his office at his headquarters beneath Derby House at Liverpool. Horton and his predecessor, Sir Percy Noble, ran the Atlantic campaign from this complex of underground chambers throughout the war.

Above, left: The plot of the Atlantic in the operations room at Derby House, showing the location of all convoys, escort groups and known concentrations of U-boats. Liverpool was a joint RN/RAF headquarters and for once inter-service rivalry was put aside in favour of getting the job done.

Above, right: A Wren plotter moves a marker on the Atlantic plot.

Below: Wrens set up an exercise in WATU – Western Approaches Tactical Unit. WATU can best be described as the 'University of the Western Approaches', where tactics were continually refined in the light of experience at sea. The officers on the course stood behind the canvas screens and were only allowed brief glimpses of the plot before making their decisions.

Above: HMS *Walker*, a member of the famous 'V&W' class of destroyers, was built in 1917 by Denny. At the beginning of the war destroyers were the only type of vessel available in any numbers for escort duty. Yet there were never enough of them and there were many other pressing calls on their services. Moreover, they were never really suited to ocean escort work – lacking endurance, they needed frequent refuelling.

Right: HMS *Shikari*, built in 1919, is seen here in 1944, by which time she had been much altered. Virtually all her gun and torpedo armament had been removed in favour of depth-charges and other anti-submarine weapons. A radar lantern on a lattice mast replaced the mainmast and the foremast is fitted with radar. All this equipment interfered with the ship's stability and there were fears for her safety in rough weather.

Right, upper: Old destroyers could be modified to act as escorts. This is HMS *Vanessa* modified as a Long Range Escort (LRE). Her forward boiler room has been converted for fuel stowage. All gun armament save two 4in and all torpedo armament have been removed to make room for depth charges and a Hedgehog ATW (Ahead Throwing Weapon). *Vanessa*'s enhanced endurance meant that she could stay with a convoy for its entire passage.

Right, lower: A 'Flower' class corvette at sea. The 'Flowers' were the first mass-produced class of escort vessel.

Below: HMS *Hotspur*, a destroyer which spent the war in the Western Approaches, is seen here in April 1945 leaving the Gladstone Dock at the start of an Atlantic voyage (though with her ensign at half mast). 'A' and 'Y' guns have been removed together with one bank of torpedo tubes – the other has been retained to fire the 1-ton depth-charge.

Top, left: Other types of vessel pressed into service as convoy escorts included trawlers such as this one, *King Sol*, seen here on the Mersey in 1944. Trawlers proved suitable as escorts because of their good seekeeping qualities, but life in such a small ship in the North Atlantic must have been miserable.

Top, centre: HMS *Broadway*, a former American vessel built in 1918 and one of the fifty destroyers leased to Britain in September 1940. These ships provided useful cover until their place could be taken by new construction.

Above, centre: HMS *Clare*, another of the former US destroyers, but virtually rebuilt as an LRE to give extra endurance.

Far left: Two *Black Swan* class sloops in Gladstone Dock at Liverpool in June 1943: HMS *Wildgoose* (outboard) and HMS *Starling* (inboard). Sloops were the most effective convoy escorts since they provided the firepower of a destroyer but on a smaller hull. However, they took too long to build and there were of course never enough of them.

Top, right: HMS *Alnwick Castle*, one of the 'Castle' class of corvettes which were larger and more seaworthy than the 'Flowers'. Armed with a 4in gun, Squid ATW and a copious supply of depth-charges, the 'Castles' were intended as stop-gaps while new frigates were built.

Above, right: Cheap and cheerful: HMS *Loch Killin* on completion. Larger than the 'Castles', the 'Lochs' carried an additional Squid ATW but were otherwise little different. Their hulls were designed for rapid prefabrication.

Below: HMS *Test*, a 'River' class frigate and the final development of the Atlantic escort.

Armament consisted of two 4in guns, a number of 20mm Oerlikons, Hedgehog ATW and 150+ depth charges. The frigates could not be completed quickly in any numbers so the 'Castle' and 'Loch' building programmes continued in tandem.

Main illustration: HMS *Duckworth*, an American-built 'Captain' class frigate, at Belfast in May 1943. The 'Captains' proved very effective submarine killers and their return to the USA after the war while the 'Lochs', 'Bays' (AA variants of the 'Loch' class) and 'Castles' were retained was not one of the best post-war procurement decisions.

Right: Ramming was the oldest and most effective anti-submarine measure. However, the resulting damage meant that the escort was out of service for some time and taking up a valuable repair berth. Ramming was therefore officially discouraged, though no officer would be disciplined for ramming a U-boat. This photograph shows damage to the bows of HMS *Viscount* after she had rammed *U661* at a speed of 26 knots on the night of 14/15 October 1942.

Far right: A fine view of HMS *Aylmer* in the Mersey in February 1945 showing the copious depth-charges carried.

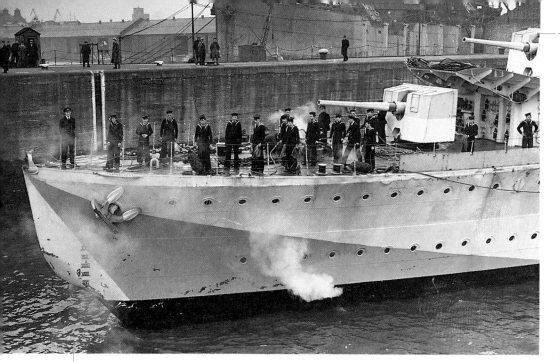

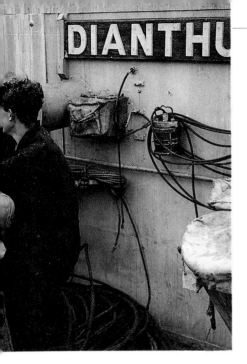

Far left, upper: Another successful ramming: this time HMS *Hesperus* enters the Gladstone Dock, Liverpool, with a damaged stem after an encounter with *U357* on 26 December 1942 during operations in support of Convoy HX.219.

Far left, lower: The consequences: the 'Captain' class frigate HMS *Aylmer* in dry dock at Holyhead after ramming *U1051* on 26 January 1945.

Left, upper: A Mk VII depth charge being loaded on to a Mk IV depth-charge thrower in the corvette HMS *Dianthus*. The depth charge, with its hydrostatic fuze, was the sole anti-submarine munition available in 1939; it could be dropped over the stern or fired from the beam.

Left, lower: Depth-charge racks on the stern of HMS *Starling*. The floats on top of the racks are Foxer decoys for use against acoustic homing torpedoes.

Below: A depth charge explodes astern of an American PC boat off the Florida coast, throwing up the characteristic plume of water. The shallower the setting, the higher the plume.

Left, top: Throughout the war the search went on for an ASW weapon that would fire a bomb ahead of the ship – the Ahead Throwing Weapon (ATW). This is one such weapon, the Fairlie Mortar – better known as the 'Five Wide Virgins' – installed for trials in HMS *Whitehall* in 1941. The weapon was not a success.

Left, centre: Hedgehog, shown here on a land test-bed, was the next development. It fired a salvo of twenty-four 65lb contact-fuzed bombs 200 yards ahead of the ship, arranged to give a 40-yards-wide impact point. Hedgehog was only really useful against shallow targets.

Left, bottom: Squid, shown here fitted in HMS *Loch Killin*, was the final such ATW. It was a three-barrelled mortar in a frame which could be rotated through 90 degrees for loading. The projectile carried a 207lb minol charge. Squid was fitted in all new-construction frigates and corvettes and its first successful use was by HMS *Loch Killin* on 31 July 1944.

Right, upper: Aircraft played a vital role in the U-boat war, in terms of both local cover for convoys and long-range patrols far out into the Atlantic. Here Wellington aircraft operate from Gibraltar out into the central Atlantic and eastwards into the Mediterranean.

Right, lower: A Sunderland Mk II flying boat of No 10 Squadron RAF used for reconnaissance and ASW operations.

Below: Bombing-up a Sunderland flying boat with a Mk XI aerial depth charge at an RAF base in West Africa.
Bottom, left: A Liberator VLR (Very Long Range) aircraft of No 200 Squadron RAF over the Azores. Liberators were among the few aircraft which could range far into the central Atlantic, an area previously beyond the reach of land-based aircraft.

Above, centre: A flare about to be dropped from a Liberator to mark the position where a U-boat has been sighted. The flare would be used as a marker for subsequent attacks.

Above, right, and below: A Leigh Light (named after its inventor) fitted to an RAF Liberator. This was a 24in naval searchlight installed in a retractable ventral housing beneath the aircraft. It had a range of 5,000 yards, and its 22 million candle watt light would illuminate a surfaced U-boat at night.

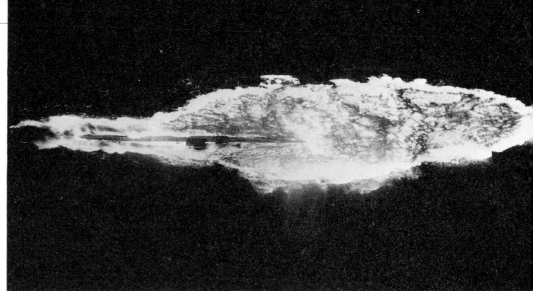

Far left, top: A Catalina flying boat of No 240 Squadron RAF. Like the Liberator, the Catalina could range far out into the Atlantic.

Far left, centre: A Martlet Mk III carrier-borne fighter. In the anti-submarine role the Martlet proved useful at AA fire-suppression while other aircraft went in with the depth charges.

Far left, bottom: The Swordfish, the maid-of-all-work of the Fleet Air Arm. For ASW duties the aircraft would be equipped with depth charges or rockets and ASV radar.

Centre, top: The USS *Card*, one of the most successful American escort carriers operating in the central Atlantic. *Card* and her sister ship *Bogue* sank eight U-boats apiece. These carriers played a vital role in providing air cover in areas beyond the reach of land-based aircraft.

Centre, above: Captain Arnold J. Isbell, USN, commanding officer of *Card*, directing operations from his carrier's island.

Right, top: A U-boat on the surface amid the depth-charge boil following an attack by *Card*'s aircraft.

Right, above: Captain F. J. Walker directs a U-boat hunt from the bridge of the sloop HMS *Starling*. Walker's name is the one most associated with the British campaign against the U-boat. Credited with sinking fourteen U-boats, he literally worked himself to death, dying suddenly in 1944.

Above, left: HMS *Starling* returning to Gladstone Dock to a tumultuous welcome on 25 February 1944 after Walker's 2nd Escort Group had sunk six U-boats in one patrol (three of the kills during a 3-hour period) in the Western Approaches.

Above, right: Captain Donald Macintyre, DSO, DSC, RN, who was responsible for the deaths of two of Germany's foremost U-boat aces, Joachim Schepke and Otto Kretschmer, on 17 March 1941.

Right, upper: The point of it all: an oil slick marks the position of a sunken U-boat. The various ships, aircraft and weapons developed by the Allies finally succeeded in beating the U-boats, though it had been a close run thing.

Right, lower: The Italian destroyer escort *Pegaso*. She was credited with sinking three British submarines, *Undaunted*, *Upholder* and *Thorn*. The Italians proved themselves extremely competent at ASW – forty-five British submarines were lost in the Mediterranean.

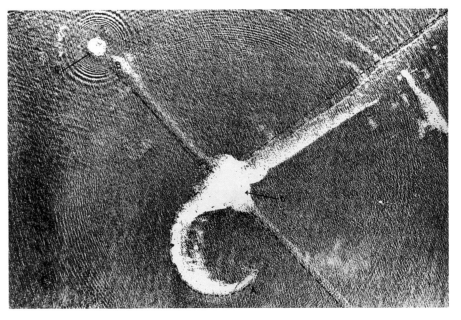

Above: A Cant Z.506B flying-boat. The slow speed and long endurance of this aircraft made it particularly suitable for ASW work.

Right, upper: A remarkable aerial reconnaissance photograph taken by an RAF Spitfire in June 1942, showing a torpedo attack on an Italian vessel by the British submarine *United*. The letter 'A' marks the track of the Italian vessel which is turning to port after being hit by the torpedo at point 'D'. The torpedo's track is indicated by the dotted line 'B'. The letter 'C' indicates *United*'s position, the ripples around this point being caused by a counter-attacking Cant Z.506B.

Right, lower: A Japanese *Kaibokan* 'B' type mass-produced escort. These ships were built as a belated attempt to counter the American submarine offensive but they came too late in the war to have any effect upon operations.

6. AMPHIBIOUS OPERATIONS

Amphibious operations were an essential part of the Allied strategy in both Europe and the Pacific. If the Germans and Japanese were to be evicted from their conquests, these areas would have to be invaded by sea and huge numbers of troops and *matériel* landed. This requirement led to the development of a new branch of naval warfare – amphibious warfare, a subject well understood by seamen in the eighteenth century but which had to be learned anew in the Second World War. The concept involved the scrupulously planned movement of hundreds of thousands of men and thousands of tons of equipment to a given place at a given time, and the Americans excelled at it. Amphibious landings provided the stepping stones to victory.

Below: British troops land in France in 1939 by ferry at a conventional harbour. In 1939 this was still the accepted way of doing things. However, the German occupation of mainland France meant that an opposed landing would be inevitable if the Germans were to be driven out of that country.

Left: The scene on the beach at Dieppe after the Anglo-Canadian attack of 19 August 1942. The raid on Dieppe was an experiment to determine whether a port could be seized and held for seventy-two hours – and it proved a costly failure: more than 3,000 troops perished in the attempt.

Below: Weary Commandos return from Dieppe. The operation had one significant consequence: any future landing would have to be made over an open beach and a whole new range of combined operations craft would be required to land the troops and equipment.

Left, upper: Amphibious exercises using LCAs (Landing Craft Assault) operating from LSIs (Landing Ships Infantry). LCAs were the smallest unit on the amphibious inventory.

Left, lower: US troops come ashore in North Africa in November 1942 – Operation 'Torch'. The landings were the first successful Anglo-American venture and showed that, only four months after Dieppe, new techniques had been developed, tested and implemented.

Right: LST 301 lands her cargo of tanks and soft-skinned vehicles on a beach in the Caribbean. The West Indies were the location for many amphibious warfare experiments.

Below: The Landing Ship Tank was the workhorse of the amphibious fleet. These remarkable craft could carry tanks, vehicles and personnel and some were even converted as hospital ships.

Left, upper: The commanding officer of LCT 367 briefs her crew before Operation 'Husky', the invasion of Sicily in June 1943. LSTs and LCTs were used for the first time in this campaign and enabled armour and vehicles to be landed over the beaches.

Left, lower: Men of the 51st Highland Division come ashore on Sicily on 9 July 1943. A total of 2,500 vessels were involved in the Sicily landings, covered by a force of 750 warships. Little opposition was encountered.

Right, upper: British armour comes ashore at Reggio on the Italian mainland on 3 September 1942. The landings on the Italian mainland were unopposed, coinciding as they did with news of the Italian surrender. However, subsequent landings at Salerno encountered stiff resistance, including the use of the German Hs 293 glider bomb, and the beachhead was only held by employing heavy naval gunfire support. The Italian landings provided essential experience for the planning of 'Overlord', the invasion of Europe.

Right, lower: Three American LCTs embark troops and vehicles of the US 1st Infantry Division at Portland destined for 'Omaha' Beach in Normandy. The invasion involved the landing of 155,000 American, British and Canadian troops on five beaches: 'Omaha' and 'Utah' (American), 'Gold' and 'Sword' (British) and 'Juno' (Canadian).

Below, left: Some idea of the scale of the operation can be gathered from this aerial view of 'Dog' and 'Easy' Beaches in the 'Omaha' sector.

Bottom, left: Men of No. 48 (Royal Marine) Commando come ashore at 'Nan Red' Beach in the area of 'Juno' near St Aubin-sur-Mer at approximately 0900 on 6 June. Many of the frail landing craft were damaged by surf and once ashore the Commandos suffered heavy casualties from the German defences.

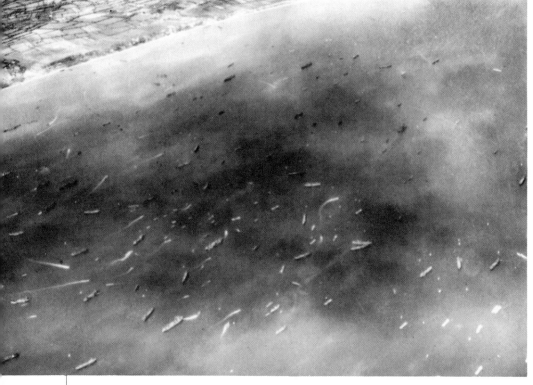

Top, centre: Second-wave troops of the 9th Canadian Infantry Brigade come ashore at 'Nan White' Beach in the 'Juno' area at Bernières-sur-Mer shortly before midday on 6 June.

Above, centre: A Royal Navy beachmaster's position in the 'Juno' area near Courseulles. The beachmasters played a vital role in ensuring the smooth movement of men and cargo from ship to shore.

Top, right: A similar US Navy position, though a good deal less comfortable than its British counterpart, on 'Utah' Beach shortly after the initial landings.

Above, right: Nothing was left to chance: officers and men of a hydrographic survey launch take a break from their surveying activities during the assault.

Left, top: A view of 'Omaha' Beach, showing LSTs discharging cargo, with shipping massed offshore.

Left, centre: The command of a large and complex amphibious operation required tailor-made facilities: it was no longer sufficient for the land forces commander to accept a 'ride' aboard the flagship of the naval commander, as had traditionally been the case. Here the American HQ ship *Ancon*, surrounded by PT boats, lies off 'Omaha' Beach in June 1944. HQ ships like *Ancon* were equipped with sophisticated command and communications systems.

Left, bottom: Probably the least glamorous but most appreciated landing craft, the Landing Barge Kitchen – seen here off 'Juno' Beach – provided a floating catering service for landing craft crews who had no cooking facilities in their little craft.

Above, centre: The cost: the graves of naval personnel buried at Bernières-sur-Mer. There were casualties among the beachmasters and the landing craft crews.

Left: Naval operations in support of the army continued after the Normandy landings. Here a naval detachment sets up camp in the Reichswald forest before the crossing of the River Rhine. The notice board, clock and loud-hailer show that barracks routine is never far away.

Above right: Naval LCAs assist in the building of a pontoon bridge over the Rhine at Xanten on 25 March 1945.

Left: American troops land on the island of New Britain on 26 December 1942. The twin-pronged American amphibious offensive in the Pacific was a vast undertaking stretching from New Guinea to the shores of Japan. New Britain was the first step in the South West Pacific Campaign and its capture gave the Americans the important port of Rabaul and the strategic base at Manus in the nearby Admiralty Islands.

Below: Some idea of the size of the American undertaking can be had from this photograph of US troops boarding the ubiquitous LST for the landings on New Britain.

Above: American troops in an LCA approach the beach at Aitape on 22 April 1944. Hollandia and Aitape fell relatively easily, but on Biak there was fierce fighting. The capture of the Dutch East Indies paved the way for the assault on the Philippines.

Below: American landing craft off the beach at Hollandia in the Dutch East Indies, April 1944.
Bottom: The first wave of landing craft carrying troops of the US Sixth Army head for the beach on the island of Leyte in the Philippines on 20 October 1944.

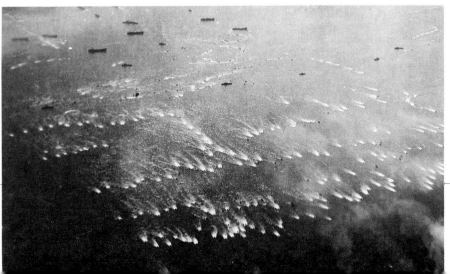

Top, left: American soldiers wade ashore at Leyte. Japanese opposition was stiff and the Americans were not helped by tropical storms. Japanese resistance ended on 28 December 1944.

Above: 'I shall return': General Douglas MacArthur makes his much publicised return to the Philippines on 20 October 1944. He was one of the few army generals with an instinctive flair for, and understanding of, amphibious operations.

Left: Logistic build-up: LSTs discharge cargo on Leyte. The Leyte landings were followed by those on the principal island of Luzon. The campaign to retake Luzon required more US troops than any other campaign of the Second World War (other than France) and was a grim battle of attrition.

Above right: While Mac-Arthur's soldiers were fighting their way up through the South West Pacific, US Marines and soldiers under the overall command of Admiral Chester Nimitz took the route through the Central Pacific to Japan. This photograph shows the waterfront at Betio on Tarawa in the Gilbert Islands, attacked in November 1943. The sea wall prevented the use of amphibious tracked vehicles and the island was only taken after a three-day struggle which cost over 1,000 American dead.

Left, top: Marines take cover on Tarawa. Possession of the Gilberts was important because it meant that an air base could be established from which attacks could be launched against the Marshall Islands, the next stage in the campaign.

Left, centre: Marines wade ashore at Saipan in the Marianas on 15 June 1944. After the Marshall Islands fell, Nimitz's forces advanced to take the Marianas, and to get there – 1,000 miles from the Marshalls – they had to assemble the largest fleet yet seen in the Pacific.

Left, bottom: Marines use a flame-thrower to deal with Japanese troops in a bunker on Saipan. The Japanese fought tenaciously and both their army and navy commanders committed suicide rather than surrender. Saipan was also the scene of mass suicides by the civilian population.

Right, upper: The 2nd Marine Division cemetery on Saipan: US casualties numbered 16,525 killed and wounded. The Marianas had fallen by mid August 1944 and preparations began for the seizure of Iwo Jima.

Right, lower: B-29 bombers on an airfield constructed on Saipan. The island quickly became a base for aircraft engaged in bombing the Japanese home islands.

Right: The first wave of landing craft heads toward the beach at Iwo Jima in the Bonins on 19 February 1945. The island was needed as a forward airfield for US fighters operating in support of bombers over Japan. In the distance can be seen the mass of Mount Suribachi which dominated the island.

Below, left: Marines unload supplies at Iwo Jima through the black volcanic ash which covered the island's surface.

Right: Jack Rosenthal's photograph showing the raising of the Stars and Stripes on Mount Suribachi sums up the gallantry of the Marines engaged in these island-hopping operations. Iwo Jima fell on 16 March and the American advance moved on the Ryuku Islands on the doorstep of Japan.

Far right: The explosion of the atomic bomb over Nagasaki on 9 August 1945 brought the Pacific War to a close and cancelled plans for an amphibious assault on Japan which would have been a bloody affair.

Left: The scene off the Hagushi beaches on the west coast of Okinawa after the landings on 1 April 1945. The Okinawa campaign was the final amphibious landing in the Pacific War and was a masterpiece of planning. The landings were unopposed, the Japanese reserving their defence until the Americans drove inland. The fighting then was fierce and the island did not fall until mid June.

7. LOGISTICS

The Second World War saw the need for the manufacture and supply of *matériel* on a scale unheard of in the history of warfare. Each side worked furiously to build ships and traditional techniques were abandoned in the quest for quantity production. Britain needed to build ships faster than they were being sunk in the Atlantic. Germany adopted mass production of U-boats late in the war and her efforts in this direction were continually frustrated by Allied bombing. Most importantly, in the United States of America the industrial might of that vast nation was mobilised to produce everything from battleships to tugs. American ingenuity triumphed over traditional practice: submarines were built on

Left: A shipbuilding yard in Britain. Even in this relatively confined area ships were built to replace the huge losses suffered in the Battle of the Atlantic.

Above: The Harland & Wolff yard at Belfast showing frigates and minesweepers under construction in the Abercorn Basin and three merchant ships on the stocks. Harland & Wolff was one of Britain's biggest shipbuilders.

Above, right: The traditional way of ship construction – riveting. This was slow and very labour intensive. Here the rivetter smooths down the rivet head with a pneumatic hammer.

Right: Riveting was gradually replaced by welding – seen here in progress on the upper deck of a destroyer – but not without considerable resistance from Britain's conservative-minded shipbuilding industry.

Left: Shipbuilding was one activity not affected by the black-out. Here welding is in progress on a warship on the Clyde at night in 1944.

Below: Soldiers from the 51st Highland Division clamber through wreckage in Hamburg's Blohm & Voss yard to inspect three Type XXI U-boats. The appointment of Albert Speer as armaments minister brought a minor revolution in German shipbuilding practice with greater emphasis placed on prefabrication. But all Speer's efforts were frustrated by the bombing offensive – note the huge crater in the foreground.

Above: USS *Missouri* goes down the ways in the traditional fashion at the New York Navy Yard on 29 January 1944. The demands of war meant that American shipbuilders would adopt more innovative methods in the quest for mass production.

the Great Lakes miles from the sea: ships were launched sideways if there were insufficient room for the more traditional method of launching, and ships were also built upside down and rotated prior to launching if it was considered easier to proceed in this fashion.

To date naval warfare had been conducted at a safe distance from a coaling station or harbour with bunkering facilities. Thus operations were constrained by the need for refuelling. The demands of operations in the Second World War changed all that. In the Atlantic there was a need for escorts that could accompany a convoy all the way across the Atlantic and not have to turn back when their fuel ran low leaving the merchant ships to proceed unescorted. There was also a requirement for escort groups to be able to remain at sea on extended operations without coming back to port to refuel. To meet this need various techniques for refuelling at sea were developed.

But it was in the Pacific that logistics became an aspect of warfare as important as front-line operations. The vast distances involved in Pacific operations meant that the Americans had to set up their own line of supply as they advanced towards

Japan. They also had to develop techniques for keeping a carrier group at sea continuously and supplied with everything from fuel and ammunition to the latest product from Hollywood.

The Allied navies not only had to learn how to keep themselves at sea, they also had to maintain armies ashore until suitable port facilities could be captured. This led to the development of unusual and imaginative techniques of re-supply. Whatever form it took, logistics was the muscle behind the Allied victory.

Below, left: A submarine-chaser being constructed upside down. When the hull was complete it would be rotated and fitted out.

Below, right: The need for landing craft was immense – they were required in huge numbers in every theatre of war. Here LCT(V)s are mass produced in a floating dock from components fabricated inland, miles from the sea. Fourteen such craft could be turned out every three weeks.

Bottom, left: One of the most remarkable stories of American shipbuilding concerns the construction of submarines at Manitowoc on the Great Lakes. The river was of insufficient width for the usual launching procedure so the spectacular sideways launch was adopted. Thirty submarines were built at here and launched in this way – this is *Puffer* being launched on 22 November 1942.

Bottom, right: After trials on Lake Michigan the submarines proceeded to the Gulf of Mexico via the Illinois Waterway and the River Mississippi – this is *Pargo* about to start her long journey to the sea. Periscopes were not fitted until the boats reached New Orleans, to enable the various bridges en route to be negotiated. Manitowoc-built boats were well regarded by submariners.

Far left, upper: Refuelling at sea: HMS *Rhododendron* experiments with the astern method from an oiler in 1943. The demands of operations required that ships be able to stay at sea for far longer periods than in the past.

Far left, lower: HMS *Warspite* fuels the destroyer HMS *Nestor* during operations off Madagascar in 1942. Larger ships were able to keep their smaller brethren 'topped up' but this was no substitute for a properly organised fleet train.

Left, upper: It was in the Pacific that replenishment at sea became essential. Here HMS *Formidable* refuels from a tanker of the British Pacific Fleet off Okinawa in May 1945. Although the destroyer is fuelling by the abeam method, the British stuck with the inefficient and slow astern method. Fuelling at sea became a nightmare for British commanders in the Pacific and nearly compromised the operational ability of the fleet.

Above, right: A seaman aboard an American tanker throws a line to a waiting destroyer. The Americans turned refuelling at sea into a fine art.

Left, lower: An American battleship receives 14in cordite charges from a 'Type Loaded' LST off Okinawa in May 1945.

Below: The nature of operations, particularly those in the Pacific, demanded that all the facilities of a major port/base in the United States be available as far forward as possible so as not to impede operations. Here a floating dock is taken sideways through the Panama Canal en route for the Pacific.

Left: An American battleship in a floating dock at Guam. The provision of such extensive repair facilities so far forward was of great importance in keeping ships operational.

Below, left: An American submarine depot ship with some of her 'flock' alongside. There were few maintenance tasks that could not be dealt with by the depot ship and her staff. The American submarine offensive was of critical importance in the defeat of Japan and its momentum was assured by

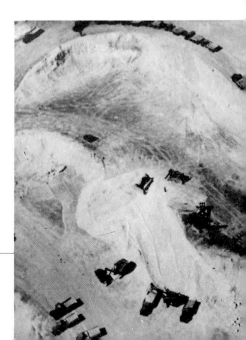

the presence of such ships which moved forward as the Americans advanced, thus cutting down the time spent on passage to and from patrol.

Below, centre: A US Navy Construction Battalion (CB) – better known as 'Seabees' – embarks for service overseas. The Seabees were a vital ingredient of the American offensive in the Pacific. After each island was taken it was transformed into a base for operations in readiness for the next objective.

Bottom, centre: An airfield under construction by Seabees on Saipan. Less than five months after the capture of the island the first B-29 Super-fortress took off from this field for a raid on Tokyo.

Right: No idle boast – this sign was erected at Torokina airfield on Bougainville.

Below: A Seabee bulldozer emerges from an LST on the Green Islands in the South Pacific. The Seabees were never far behind the combat troops.

So when we reach the
"Isle of Japan"
With our caps at a
Jaunty tilt
We'll enter the city of Tokyo
On the roads the SEABEES
Built.

Third Marine Div.
2ND Raider Reg.

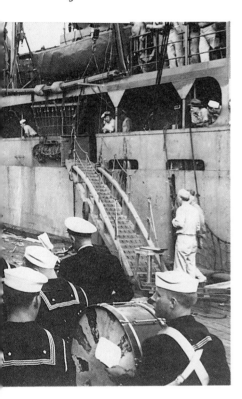

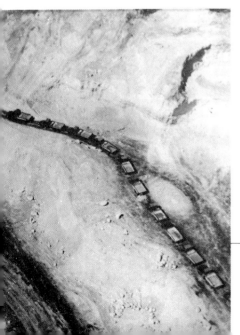

Above: Supplies being unloaded on the dockside by British merchant ships – in this case at Cyprus. The Allies depended on moving supplies by sea for the maintenance of the various offensives.
Below: The long US supply lines to Europe and the Pacific.
Right, upper: A huge fleet of merchant ships unloads supplies at Saipan in 1945.
Right, lower: The harbour at Guam, showing the immense storage facilities available.

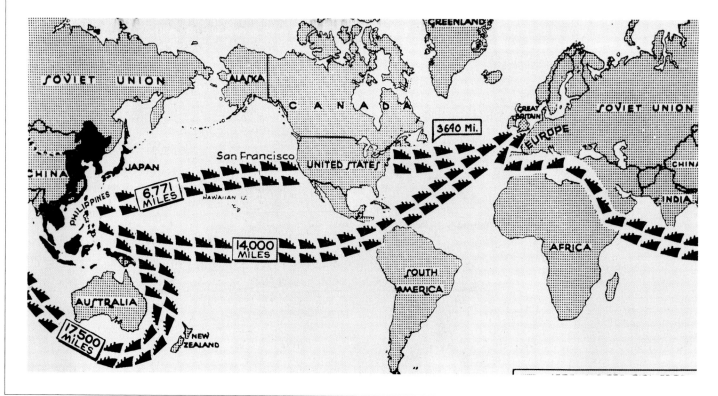

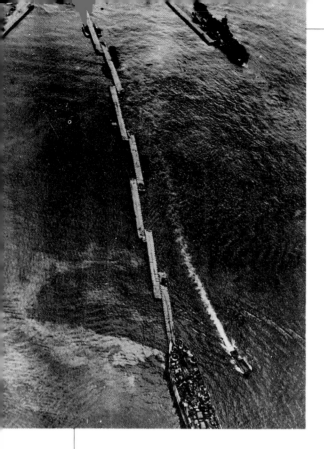

Above, left: Where harbours did not exist – and this was the case in most of the Pacific islands captured by the Americans – they would be built. This is a pontoon causeway constructed into deep water by Seabees at Leyte in 1944.

Above, centre: The Mulberry Harbour at Arromanches. Mulberry was certainly the most audacious logistic development to keep an army supplied in the field.

Below: A 'Whale' causeway for one of the Mulberry harbours being towed into position. 'Whales' ran from the pierhead to the shore. In the background are the concrete caissons and blockships which sheltered the anchorage.

Above, far right: The pierhead at a Mulberry Harbour, showing the legs which allowed the platform to move up and down with the tide, permitting operations to continue twenty-four hours a day.

Right: A pierhead in use with ambulances taking wounded to the hospital ship *St Dinard*. The upper level of the pierhead allowed loading and unloading to be carried on at two levels, hastening turn-around time.

Above, left: Coasters discharging over the beach at Arromanches. The effectiveness of Mulberry has been disputed, particularly after Mulberry 'A' on Utah Beach was wrecked by the great gale in June 1944; many thought that discharge directly over the beach was quicker. Nevertheless, Mulberry remains an outstanding and imaginative achievement.

Below, left: One of the greatest and most pressing needs of the Allied armies in North-West Europe was fuel to sustain the large numbers of tanks, trucks and other vehicles – the war in that theatre being more mechanised than the island-hopping campaign in the Pacific. Supply of case petrol over the beaches was one answer, but the proximity of the British Isles led to a more imaginative solution being adopted: PLUTO – Pipe Line Under the Ocean – a submarine pipeline linking southern England with France. This is the pipeline wound on to

its bobbin, known as a 'Conun–drum'.

Below, centre: The 'Conun–drum' is towed across the channel, paying out the cable as it goes. The secret of PLUTO had been well kept and the sight of the 'Conundrum' caused consternation and disbelief in the assault area.

Above, right: The control station in the UK. The board shows delivery states of petrol and kerosene. Further pipelines were laid as the Allied advance progressed. Deliveries by pipeline were not suspended until the port of Antwerp had been captured.

Below, right: No aspect of logistics was left unattended to. Mail was of vital importance in maintaining morale. Here US Marine Corps technicians process microfilmed V-Mail on Saipan. The service was introduced in mid 1942 and in two years the US Army and Navy postal services handled 789,539,390 V-Mail letters.

Right: Admiral Sir Dudley Pound (1877–1943), First Sea Lord and executive head of the Royal Navy during the first three years of the war when things were at their worst. Although criticised as an arch-centraliser, Pound was an effective commander who stood up to Churchill and fought his service's corner. He was also a calm and steadying influence at a time when losses were heavy and the Royal Navy was stretched to the limit. He died in office in 1943 and it is unfortunate that his many sterling qualities have been overshadowed by the PQ.17 controversy.

Left: Pound was replaced by Admiral Sir Andrew Cunningham (1883–1963), who came fresh from his triumphs in the Mediterranean. Popularly known as 'ABC', Cunningham was unusual in that he had never before held a major appointment. He was a commander rather than an administrator and the complete antithesis to Pound. He remains the outstanding British naval commander of the Second World War.

Left: Admiral Sir John Tovey (1885–1971), Commander-in-Chief Home Fleet 1940–43. Tovey was an able commander who masterminded the hunt for and sinking of the *Bismarck*. He was, however, in a state of almost perpetual disagreement with Churchill.

Below, left: Tovey's successor was Admiral Sir Bruce Fraser (1888–1984), a convivial individual whose charm concealed a sharp analytical mind. His main achievements were the sinking of the *Scharnhorst* in December 1943 and his command of the British Pacific Fleet in 1944–45.

Below, right: Vice-Admiral Sir James Somerville, a fighting admiral who commanded the famous Force H in the Mediterranean, and subsequently the Eastern Fleet. A competent and popular commander, and another of the British admirals who fell foul of Churchill.

Left: Admiral Sir Percy Noble addresses the crew of HMS *Stork* after their sinking of *U574*. Noble was the first Commander-in-Chief Western Approaches, a command instituted to control the Atlantic convoys. He did sterling work in organising his command before moving to Washington to head the British naval mission, and his careful work has often been overshadowed by his more ebullient successor.

Below left: Admiral Sir Max Horton (1883–1951), Great War submariner and *bon viveur*, who succeeded Noble as CinC Western Approaches. He combined charm with utter ruthlessness. His headquarters were a model of efficiency and inter-service co-operation, and he can justly be described as the victor of the Battle of the Atlantic.

Left: Rear-Admiral Robert Burnett. Not one of the Navy's intellectuals, Burnett was a superb fighting commander who was never happier than when in the thick of things. He fought Convoy PQ.18 through to Russia in September 1942, commanded British forces at the Battle of the Barents Sea and commanded the cruiser squadron at the Battle of the North Cape. He was dearly loved by all who served with him.

Left: Admiral Sir Bertram Ramsay, one of the least known British naval commanders. After his organisation of the Dunkirk evacuation in 1940, Ramsay planned the landings in North Africa, Italy and North-West Europe with meticulous care. His death in an air accident in 1944 robbed the Navy of an outstanding commander.
Right: Admiral Sir Henry Harwood (1888–1950). He commanded British forces at the Battle of the River Plate in 1939, but showed little promise in subsequent appointments. His handling of the June 1942 convoy to Malta, Operation 'Vigorous', is particularly open to question.

Left, top: Grand Admiral Erich Raeder (1876–1960), Commander-in-Chief of the German Navy. His plans for a large surface fleet had not been fulfilled when war was declared. The ineffectiveness of Germany's surface fleet, which was not his fault, lost him Hitler's support and he resigned in January 1943 after the fiasco of the Battle of the Barents Sea. He was sentenced to life imprisonment at Nuremberg, but was released early on compassionate grounds.

Left, centre: Raeder was succeeded by Admiral Karl Dönitz (1891–1984), who had commanded the U-boat fleet with distinction and thus won Hitler's approval. It was largely thanks to his very personal style of leadership that morale held up in the U-boat arm despite the fearful losses. One of his lesser known achievements was the successful evacuation of thousands of refugees from East Prussia in the teeth of the Red Army.

Left, bottom: Vice-Admiral Otto Ciliax, the German commander who led the successful 'Channel Dash' in February 1942.

Top, right: Vice-Admiral Gunther Lütjens (1889–1941) commanded *Scharnhorst* and *Gneisenau* on their commerce raiding foray into the Atlantic in March 1941 and also the *Bismarck* group two months later. By May 1941 Lütjens, a very capable officer, was worn out and his conduct during the *Bismarck*'s brief sortie reveals several errors of judgement. His continued employment was a sign that the German Navy lacked young and vigorous tactical commanders. He did not survive the sinking of the *Bismarck*.

Above: Admiral Isoroku Yamamoto (1884–1943), Japanese strategist who planned the attack on Pearl Harbor. Yamamoto lacked the insularity common to many Japanese commanders and feared the immense industrial might of the United States. He is quoted as saying after the Pearl Harbor operation: 'I fear all we have done is rouse a sleeping giant and fill him with a terrible resolve.' He was killed in a brilliantly executed air ambush in 1943, but his reputation as the first practitioner of carrier warfare is secure.

Above, left: Admiral Ernest J. King (1878–1956), American Chief of Naval Operations – a cold and forbidding individual, but one whose conduct of policy in Washington left his commanders at sea free to fight their battles. Often known as an Anglophobe, King should best be remembered for the brilliance of his logistic arrangements and his strategic direction of the war against Japan.

Above, centre: Admiral William 'Bull' Halsey (1882–1959), an erratic genius whose brilliance and flair for publicity concealed some serious operational shortcomings. His invigorating optimism and aggressiveness (slogans such as 'Kill Japs! Kill Japs! Kill More Japs!') sustained the US Navy greatly during the grim early months of 1942

Above, right: Vice-Admiral Raymond Spruance (1886–1969), American commander at Midway (Halsey being stricken with dermatitis). Spruance had the reputation of being a careful commander who would not take risks lightly but yet who would strike decisively when required. He was a meticulous planner whose operations nearly always turned out as he expected. If not as dashing as Halsey, he is best remembered as coolly competent and highly successful.

Below: Vice-Admiral Marc A. Mitscher (1887–1947) was a superb American practitioner of carrier warfare. In 1944 he commanded Task Force 58, the fast carrier group which participated in the battles of Truk, the Philippine Sea, Leyte Gulf, Iwo Jima and Okinawa. His thorough understanding of naval aviation and his relaxed attitude towards the small print of naval regulations won him the affection of his crews.

Left, upper: Rear-Admiral Richmond Kelly Turner (1885–1961), American master of amphibious warfare. He directed the landings at Tarawa, the Marshalls, Iwo Jima and Okinawa. No aspect of an amphibious landing was too small for his attention.

Left, lower: Rear-Admiral John S. McCain (1884–1945), known as 'Slew' or 'Popeye' on account of his sunken cheeks and prominent nose, was an aviator who held the posts of Chief of Bureau of Aeronautics from 1942 to August 1943, Deputy Chief of Naval Operations (Air) from August 1943 to July 1944 and Commander Second Carrier Task Force from July 1944 to August 1945 (a post in which he alternated command with Mitscher) – despite coming to naval aviation fairly late in his career. He was fearless, aggressive, showy, profane and occasionally hot-headed. He is perhaps best remembered for his work overseeing the development and training of carrier task forces and their shoreside support while DCNO (Air). By the end of the war he was in poor health due to overwork and he died on 6 September 1945.

Right, upper: Rear-Admiral Frederick ('Fightin' Freddie') Sherman, a carrier task group commander who succeeded Mitscher in command of the First Fast Carrier Task Force in the Pacific in July 1945, having spent the war entirely in naval aviation. He was an extrovert character and a superb tactician, and he loved a good fight.

Right, lower: Vice-Admiral Willis A. Lee (1888–1945) was the US Navy's premier battleship force commander during the war. Lee was appointed to a battleship shortly after graduating from USNA in 1908 and thereafter served continuously in ships of that type. After six months as King's Chief of Staff he went to the Pacific in August 1942 as commander of a battleship division and saw action in the Second Battle of Guadalcanal when ships under his command sank the Japanese battleship *Kirishima* on the night of 14/15 November 1942. Thereafter he served as Commander Battleships Pacific Fleet and Commander Battleship Squadron Two. His ships supported the carrier strikes and amphibious assaults of the US Central Pacific Campaign. He died on 25 August 1945 while in the USA advising on the development of anti-*Kamikaze* tactics.

Left, upper: Admiral Thomas C. Kinkaid (1888–1972) was one of the US Navy's most widely experienced naval commanders, who served under Halsey as a carrier group commander and from November 1943 commanded the Seventh Fleet in the South-West Pacific under MacArthur. He fought in all the major battles of the first year of the Japanese war, including Coral Sea, Midway and the Guadalcanal Campaign. He later oversaw operations in the Aleutians. He performed ably and professionally as Commander Seventh Fleet, avoiding confrontation with MacArthur. He was also able to cajole Nimitz into parting with resources for his theatre of operations against the counsel of those in his own service who would not 'trust' MacArthur with fast carriers and modern battleships.

Left, lower: Vice-Admiral Alan G. Kirk (1888–1963) was the senior US Navy commander in the European theatre. After a background in naval intelligence, he served two terms as Naval Attaché in London before assuming command of the Atlantic Fleet's amphibious forces in February 1943. He oversaw operations in Sicily in 1943 and in Normandy in June 1944. In the latter operation his decision to launch landing craft as much as eleven miles offshore was much criticised at the time. After the conclusion of the Normandy Campaign he was appointed to command all naval forces in France. He retired in 1946 but continued to serve his country in a number of diplomatic appointments.

Right, upper: Vice-Admiral Charles A. Lockwood (left; seen here meeting airmen rescued by the submarine *Tang* in 1944) commanded the US Pacific Fleet's submarine force and from 7 December 1941 until the Japanese capitulation he waged an unrelenting war against Japanese shipping. Although Lockwood is not as well known as many of the more flamboyant carrier commanders, the operations of the submarines under his command were responsible for the destruction of the Japanese merchant marine and the strangulation of the Japanese war economy. A dynamic leader, Lockwood was familiar with every aspect of his command and he inspired those who served under him.

Right, lower: Fleet Admiral William D. Leahy (1875–1959). Although in official retirement at the outbreak of the Second World War, Leahy returned to duty, first as US Ambassador to Vichy France and from June 1942 as Chief of Staff to President Roosevelt and *de facto* Chairman of the Joint Chief of Staff Committee. In this last appointment he demonstrated great tact in dealing with his strong-minded colleagues and in relations with the British, and for his service in this appointment he was the first of seven senior officers to be appointed to five-star rank in December 1944. After four more years in the White House under President Truman, Leahy retired for a second time.

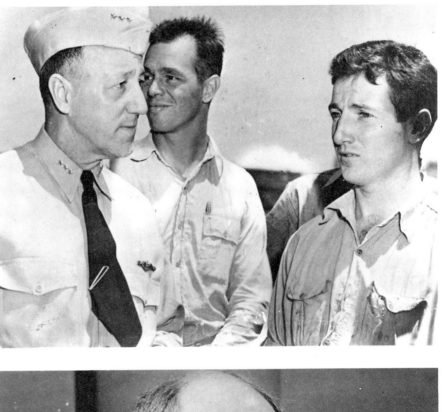

9. MIDGET SUBMARINES

During the Second World War the major belligerent navies with the exception of the USA, France and the USSR employed midget submarines, fast motor boats or specially trained assault frogmen. The absence of France from this field is easily explained – her capitulation in June 1940 effectively removed her from the war. The USA possessed conventional forces in abundance and so did not need to resort to this form of warfare. The absence of the Soviet Union from this area of operations is puzzling, given the pioneering work done by Russian engineers in submarine development, but perhaps the highly individualistic nature of midget submarine operations is not one that would have sat easily alongside the centralised Soviet command structure.

Three kinds of midget submarine made their appearance during the Second World War: human

Below: *HA-19* washed ashore on the island of Oahu after the Japanese attack on Pearl Harbor on 7 December 1941. Five *Ko-Hyoteki* attacked the harbour at the same time as the aircraft and great things were expected of them but all five were lost. Two penetrated the defences but were sunk inside the harbour, one was never found, the fourth sank outside the harbour and the fifth, *HA-19*, was attacked by the destroyer *Ward* before striking a reef and drifting ashore. Her commanding officer, Ensign Kazuo Sakamaki, was captured and became America's first PoW.

Above: As the American advance drew near the Home Islands the Japanese resorted to the mass production of midget submarines in a last-ditch attempt to prevent invasion. This photograph shows a building dock at Kure packed with Type D *Ko-Hyoteki*s, better known as the *Koryu* (Scaly Dragon). These craft could be built at a rate of 180 a month, but American bombing and shortage of raw materials meant that of the 540 ordered in June 1944, only 115 were completed.

torpedoes (the Italian *Maiale* and British Chariot); small submersibles (the German *Neger* and associated craft and the Japanese *Kaiten*) and true midget submarines (the Japanese *Ko-Hyoteki*, the Italian CA/CB types, the British X-Craft and the German *Seehund*). These craft can also be further divided into the practical and therefore successful (British X-Craft, Italian *Maiale*); those that were enthusiastically designed but impracticable (British Chariot, Japanese *Ko-Hyoteki*, German *Biber*) and the suicidal, either by accident or by design (British Welman, German *Neger*, Japanese *Kaiten* and its various derivatives).

It was the Italians who led the way with the development of the two-man human torpedo, the *Maiale*, which were used to such deadly effect at Alexandria and Gibraltar. The activities of the Italian CA/CB midget submarines are less well known but are worthy of attention, particularly the operation to attack shipping in New York, an operation that would have had the most serious effects in America but which was cancelled at the Italian armistice.

Japan was another of the early pioneers in this field. Before the war the Japanese developed the excellent two-man *Ko-Hyoteki*, an extremely advanced midget submarine. Japanese war plans concentrated on the great battleship engagement between the American and Japanese fleets which would decide the course of the war. To whittle down the American superiority in capital ship, *Ko-Hyotekis* were to launch mass torpedo attacks. It was an ingenious idea and might well have

Left, upper: The most significant success for the *Ko-Hyoteki* was the attack on HMS *Ramillies* at Diego Suarez in May 1942; one torpedo from Lieutenant Saburo Akeida's craft put the battleship out of action for nearly a year. Thereafter these little craft were employed in coastal defence as the American advance rampaged across the Pacific. It was a largely fruitless task: most, like these two found at Kiska in the Aleutians in June 1943, were destroyed by the Americans before they could be used.

Left, lower: The *Kaiten* (Heaven Shaker) was another 'answer' to Japan's crisis. This was a manned version of the Type 93 Long Lance torpedo, armed with a 1,550kg warhead. *Kaitens* could be launched over the sterns specially adapted vessels, as shown here, or carried by parent submarines. The weapon had a crude periscope and the operator simply pointed the vessel at the target and accelerated to speeds of more than 30 knots. Early *Kaitens* had a means for the operator to escape before impact, though most operators preferred to die for their Emperor. Later models were purely suicide weapons.

worked. But the Japanese decision to destroy the US fleet by a carrier strike removed their *raison d'être*. Instead they were employed in harbour penetration – a task for which they were not suited and at which they were less than successful. As the tide of war went against Japan, the Japanese resorted to suicide weapons such as the *Kaiten* and *Kairyu*. These were intended to overwhelm the Americans by sheer weight of numbers, but once deployed these craft proved no match for the range of anti-submarine measures employed by the Americans.

It was Italian activities in the Mediterranean that spurred the British into the field. Britain had traditionally made no attempt to develop this sort of weapon – since the Royal Navy was the pre-eminent

Top, left: The oiler *Mississinewa* burning at Ulithi on 20 November 1944. Five *Kaiten*s were launched by the submarines *I36* and *I47* to attack the large number of ships in the anchorage. The defences were alert and only one struck home, sinking *Mississinewa* with the loss of 150 of her crew. The only other *Kaiten* victim was the destroyer USS *Underhill* on 24 July 1945, although it is not clear whether the *Kaiten* struck the destroyer or whether *Underhill* rammed the *Kaiten*.

Top, right: *Kaiten*s mounted on the casing of the Japanese *I370* as she sails to attack American shipping on 20 February 1945. The *Kaiten* crews, wearing their traditional *Hachimaki* headbands and carrying swords, are standing on their craft. Six days later *I370* was sunk off Iwo Jima by the destroyer *Finnegan*, her *Kaiten*s unused.

Above, left: A Japanese two-man *Kairyu* at Kure in September 1945. This was the only Japanese midget submarine designed specifically for suicide missions. It was armed with either two 18in torpedoes or a 600kg explosive charge. The war ended before these craft could be used operationally.

Top, left: The Italian *Maiale* ('Pig') two-man human torpedo, more officially known as the *Siluro a lenta Corsa* (slow-running torpedo). Based on the *Mignatta* of the First World War, these craft were operated by the *Decima Mas* (10th Light Flotilla); they carried a 300lb warhead which was placed beneath the target's hull, suspended by cables from clamps attached to the bilge keel. The crew, wearing diving suits and breathing oxygen, sat astride the vessel.
Above, left: The Italian tanker *Olterra* at Gibraltar. Gibraltar became the focus for an un-remitting offensive by Italian human torpedoes and assault frogmen from the beginning of the war until the Italian armistice. The first two attacks were launched from a submarine, but subsequently *Olterra*, which was supposedly 'interned' at Algeciras, was converted to act as a forward base with the tacit connivance of the Spanish authorities. *Olterra* had an exit/re-entry compartment for the *Maiale* and she was the base from which two attacks were launched on Gibraltar in which more than 40,000 tons of shipping were lost.
Above, right: HMS *Queen Elizabeth* at anchor behind the nets at Alexandria. The greatest single success of the *Maiale* was the attack on Alexandria on the night of 18/19 December 1941, led by *Capitano di Corvetta* de la Penne. Three *Maiale* were launched and all found targets: the battleships HMS *Valiant* and *Queen Elizabeth* were badly damaged: *Valiant* was out of action for seven months, but *Queen Elizabeth* needed nearly eighteen months in dock for the

naval force in the world there was no need. It was only the need to attack the German battleship *Tirpitz* which pushed a reluctant Admiralty in this direction. With the Chariot, the British initially copied the Italian two-man human torpedo, but these craft proved unsuccessful and never justified the time and resources spent on them. Far more successful was the X-Craft, a four-man midget submarine which could be put to a variety of uses and was a most potent weapon of war. At the other end of the scale was the Welman, a useless craft whose design shows the effects of allowing enthusiasm to triumph over practicality. British midgets saw action in all three theatres of war; their most significant success was the crippling of the *Tirpitz* in September 1943.

The Germans were the last into the field. While the U-boats were scoring significant successes in the Atlantic, the *Kriegsmarine* showed no interest in these craft. Only when the Germans were confronted with the prospect of an Allied invasion of Europe did their attitude change, but in this they mirrored the Japanese, and were tacitly admitting that their naval strategy had failed. German midgets were weapons of desperation, founded in the hope that if used in sufficient numbers they would interrupt the Allied cross-Channel supply lines. With the exception of the excellent *Seehund* two-man submarine, German midgets were poorly constructed and most were as

damage to be made good. Other casualties included the oiler *Sagona* and the destroyer HMS *Jervis*. Six men and three human torpedoes had changed the balance of power in the Mediterranean overnight.
Right: Italian interest in midget submarines did not stop with human torpedoes. This photograph shows the midget submarine *CB-5* at Costanza on the Black Sea in May 1942. These four-man craft were developed from the CA class prototype and twenty-two were built of a projected seventy-two.

They were armed with two 21in torpedoes, but four mines could be carried as an alternative. *CB-1* to *CB-6* were sent to the Black Sea, where among their other successes they sank three Soviet submarines. *CB-5* was sunk by Soviet aircraft at Yalta on 13 June 1942; the others were all eventually handed over to the Romanians.

Left, top: Two CB class midgets captured at Taranto in September 1943. The external stowage for the two torpedoes is visible. Three of the remaining fourteen CBs were captured by the Allies, the rest being employed by the Italian Social Republic, Mussolini's fascist government in northern Italy. All had fairly lively careers and only three survived the war.

Left, centre: The well in the casing of the submarine *Leonardo da Vinci*, to carry a CA class submarine across the Atlantic for an attack on shipping inside the harbour at New York. This was undoubtedly the most daring midget submarine operation ever planned, and its success would have had psychological consequences out of all proportion to any damage done. The Italian armistice caused the operation to be cancelled and it remains one of the most intriguing 'what ifs?' of the Second World War.

Left, bottom: The Chariot was the British response the activities of *Decima Mas*. It was virtually identical, having been copied from a *Maiale* fished out of Gibraltar harbour. The two-man crew faced forward, the 'driver' sitting in the forward position with the 'Number Two' behind, who would help guide the craft through nets or other obstacles. The chariot's weapon was a 600lb charge, carried in the 'nose', which would be laid beneath the target.

Below, left: The driver's position in a Chariot, showing the controls. In the centre is the 'helm' which operated the rudder and hydroplanes, with a magnetic compass fitted in front of it. The switches to the left and right of the helm were for ballast pumps; the handle behind the helm is for the main motor. For security, the censor has obliterated the markings on two of the gauges.

Below, right: A 'Charioteer' being dressed in his Sladen Suit (after Commander Geoffrey Sladen who designed it, but better known as the 'Clammy Death' suit). The breathing apparatus, visible on the diver's chest, was based on the Davis Submarine Escape Apparatus, in general use throughout the fleet, and relied on oxygen being recycled through a Protosorb unit. Unfortunately not much was known about the hazards of breathing oxygen under pressure and there were a number of fatalities.

lethal to their crews as they were intended to be to the opposition.

Fast explosive motor-boats were employed by Italy, Germany and Japan. In the case of the first two countries, the operator was provided with a means to get clear before the boat exploded, but the Japanese *Shinyo* craft were true suicide weapons. The crucial factor in the employment of these craft was surprise. If the opposition could be caught napping these little craft could deliver a significant blow – as the Italians did at Suda Bay in March 1941. But if sent against defences which were alert and equipped with the all-seeing eye of radar, the craft were on virtual death ride, as the Italians found out at Malta.

In looking at midget submarine operations during the Second World War, the following conclusions can be drawn. First, midget submarines have the capacity to inflict massive blows on the enemy. Secondly, they are cheap and easy to build, and, once built, are easy to conceal. Thirdly, no harbour defences, however strong, have ever stopped a midget submarine attack: to alter slightly the famous quotation of Prime Minister Stanley Baldwin, 'The midget submarine will

always get through.' Fourthly, the threat of attack by midget craft can tie up large numbers of forces to guard against such a threat. The crucial factor in the success of these craft is the quality of the personnel rather than *matériel*. A special type of man is required for these operations and he must have exceptional qualities of determination together with professional skills of a high order. The operations of the various midget submarines during the Second World War remain some of the supreme examples of cold-blooded courage in history. Following the failure of the Japanese attack on Sydney, Rear-Admiral Stuart Muirhead-Gould, in charge of the harbour defences at Sydney, paid the following tribute to the Japanese officers and men who had perished in the attack:

'Theirs was a courage which is not the property, or the tradition or the heritage of any one nation. It is the courage shared by the brave men of our own countries as well of the enemy and, however horrible war and its results may be, it is courage which is recognised and universally admired. These men were patriots of the highest order. How many of us are really prepared to make one thousandth of the sacrifice these men have made?'

Those words are a fitting epitaph for all such men.

Below, left: Chariots were carried to their targets in pressure-tight containers on the casing of larger submarines. This photograph shows HMS *Trooper* fitted with two such containers on her after casing. *Trooper*, together with HMS *Thunderbolt* and *P-311*, took part in Operation 'Principal' on the night of 2/3 January 1943, simultaneous attacks on La Maddalena in Sardinia and Palermo in Sicily. The result was damage to the light cruiser *Ulpio Traiano* and the liner *Viminale* at Palermo, but *P-311* was lost, believed mined, off La Maddalena. Taken together with the loss of HMS *Traveller* during a pre-attack reconnaissance of Taranto, the operation can at best be described as a qualified success – two operational submarines sunk and their crews killed in exchange for damage to an Italian cruiser (which was not going to do anyone any harm) and a liner was not particularly advantageous.

Right, upper: : A spin-off from Chariot operations was the 'Sleeping Beauty', a motorised canoe which could dive to a depth of 40 feet while carrying six limpet mines in addition to the operator's equipment. Sleeping Beauties were used only once, for an attack on Singapore in October 1944 but they were discovered by the Japanese before the attack could be launched. Fourteen of the attackers were killed and ten captured, of whom one subsequently died in captivity. The remaining nine went before a Japanese court-martial and, after the inevitable guilty verdict, were beheaded one week before the Japanese surrender.

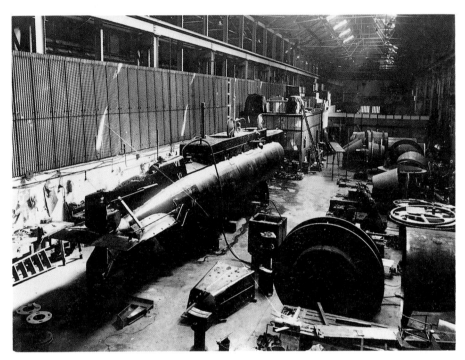

Left: In the Mk II Chariot, shown here, the operators sat back to back in a cockpit rather than astride the craft. Mk IIs were used in a rather pointless attack on two Italian-flag merchant ships at Phuket, Thailand, on 27 October 1944, mounted probably to demonstrate the craft's capabilities to the Americans. Thereafter Chariots were not employed in the Far East for fear of what the Japanese would do to a captured Charioteer.

Above: The best known and most successful British midget submarine was the X-Craft, shown here under construction at the Huddersfield works of Thomas Broadbent in 1944. True miniature submarines carrying a crew of four (commanding officer, First Lieutenant, engineer and diver), they were driven by conventional diesel-electric propulsion and armed with two 3,570lb charges of amatol, carried one on each side, which were laid beneath the target. They had a 'Wet and Dry' compartment whence a diver could leave the boat to deal with obstacles (special net cutters were carried in lockers in the casing) or plant limpet mines. The first prototypes were in service at the end of 1942 and the operational craft shortly thereafter.

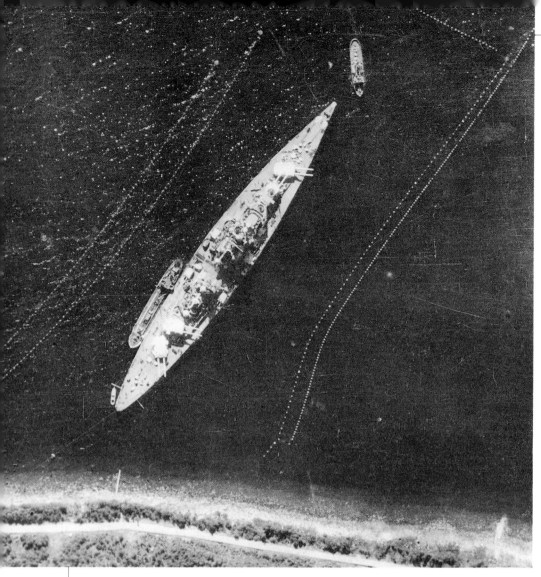

Left: The German battleship *Tirpitz*, known as the 'Lone Queen of the North' but perhaps better described by Churchill as 'The Beast', lying behind her nets at Kaafiord. Although inactive, *Tirpitz* exercised an influence on British planning that was totally disproportionate. The Admiralty resolved that she should be eliminated, and, since *Tirpitz* was beyond the reach of conventional forms of attack, something different had to be tried. There had been an attempt to use Chariots in November 1942 but this had failed. Now the newly constructed X-Craft were to be given an opportunity.

Below, left: HMS *Thrasher* tows *X-5* out to sea on 11 September 1943 to begin Operation 'Source', the attack on *Tirpitz*. Six X-Craft were involved (*X-5* to *X-10*) but only *X-6* (Lieutenant Donald Cameron) and *X-7* (Lieutenant Geoffrey Place) managed to get their cargoes beneath the target. Of the other three, *X-5* disappeared and *X-8*

and *X-9* were lost on passage. The commanding officer of *X-10* took the morally courageous decision to withdraw after his boat developed so many mechanical problems that to carry on might mean compromising the operation. Nevertheless, the damage done to *Tirpitz* by Cameron and Place effectively ended her career as a sea-going unit of the *Kriegsmarine* and both men were deservedly awarded the Victoria Cross – an award they would have to wait for until their return from a prisoner-of-war camp.

Below, centre: *X-24* at Loch Cairnbawn, flying her 'Jolly Roger' after a successful mission to Bergen under the command of Lieutenant Max Shean, RANVR on 13 April 1944 in which the 7,500-ton merchant ship *Barenfels* was sunk. But Shean's intended target had been the nearby floating dock, so in September 1944 Lieutenant Percy West-macott took *X-24* back to complete the job.

Above, left: *X-23*, commanded by Lieutenant George Honour, RNR, returns to the HQ ship HMS *Largs* on 6 June, having, together with *X-20* (Lieutenant K. Hudspeth, RANVR) spear-headed the invasion fleet by some 48 hours in order to act as navigational beacons for the flights of landing craft heading toward 'Juno' and 'Sword' Beaches. For this purpose both craft were fitted with a navigational beacon on a folding mast (not visible here) and each flew a white ensign of a size normally reserved for capital ships so that there should be no mistaking their identity. Before the invasion, both craft had participated in Operation 'Postage Able', a close reconnaissance of the likely landing beaches in the Seine Bay.

Above, right: *XE-6* on trials in Rothesay Bay in August 1944. XE-Craft were a variant of the original design produced specially for service in the Far East. As the war in Europe drew to a close, six XE-Craft were deployed to the Far East where there appeared to be no shortage of potential targets. But before they could go into action they had to overcome a considerable amount of suspicion from the Americans about their capabilities.

Left, top: The Japanese cruiser *Takao*, the main target for *XE-3* and *XE-1* in Operation 'Struggle'. *XE-3*, commanded by Lieutenant I. E. Fraser, RNR, successfully placed limpet mines on *Takao*'s hull but then became jammed under the cruiser's bilge keel because of the falling tide. Desperate manoeuvring extricated the craft, but, having dropped one side cargo, Fraser found that the second would not release. *XE-3*'s diver, Leading Seaman Magennis, left the boat for a second time and prised the charge free with a crowbar. Meanwhile *XE-1*, which was to place her charges under *Takao*'s sister ship *Myoko*, was running behind schedule, so her commanding officer, Lieutenant Smart, RNR, placed his side cargoes under *Takao* as well. *Takao* was damaged beyond repair. Both Fraser and Magennis were awarded the Victoria Cross for this episode.

Left, centre: HMS *Selene* preparing to take *XE-5* in tow at Subic Bay in July 1945. *XE-5* was ordered to cut the Hong Kong/Singapore telegraph cable after *XE-4* had shown that such an operation was possible by cutting the Saigon/Singapore/Hong Kong cables on 31 July. *XE-5* was not so fortunate: she spent three and a half days searching for the cable, her diver often working up to his shoulders in white mud. The operation was abandoned, but after the war it was learned that *XE-5*'s nosing about in the mud had, in fact, damaged the cable so that it was unusable. This low-level operation, the disruption of the enemy's strategic communications, was a perfect example of what the X-Craft could achieve.

Left, bottom: XE-Craft awaiting demolition at Sydney after the war. There was little use for midget submarines in the post-war fleet where 'austerity' was the order of the day. Three XEs were retained until 1952 and were then replaced by four *X-51* class, but eventually the demands of economy prevailed and all had paid off by 1958.

Right, upper: In total contrast to the X-Craft was the British Welman one-man submarine. Designed and built by a group of enthusiastic amateurs at SOE (Special Operations Executive, charged with the organisation of sabotage and resistance in occupied Europe) with no reference to the Navy's vast reservoir of knowledge of submarine construction, the Welman broke virtually every unwritten law of midget submarine design. The craft was armed with a 1,190lb warhead in the nose, which would be laid beneath the target. The Welmans were only used once operationally, in an attack on Bergen in November 1943 in which all four craft were lost. Subsequently the Navy advised that no further use be found for these craft.

Right, lower: The Welfreighter, a two-man submersible based on the Welman and designed for the covert insertion and maintenance of special forces ashore. This view is looking forward from the port quarter and shows the cargo 'well' aft of the conning tower. The cargo was stored in six cylinders and the transom could be folded down and the cargo simply floated ashore. Unlike its predecessor, the Welfreighter did have a future, but hostilities ended in the Balkans and the Far East before these craft could be deployed.

Left, top: A German *Neger* (Nigger), one of the first such weapons deployed by the *Kriegsmarine*. It was extremely primitive, consisting of one G7e torpedo slung beneath another which had been modified to carry the operator. It could not dive but ran awash towards the target before releasing the torpedo, which fell free and commenced its run; there were occasions on which the torpedo failed to release from the carrier and dragged the whole craft to destruction. *Neger* operators were not suicide men, although their survival odds were realistically quoted as 50:50.

Left, centre: The operator sitting in his position in a *Neger*. He was equipped with closed-cycle Drager breathing apparatus, a wrist compass, a few rudimentary controls and little else. He sat too low to see his target properly and in any case his canopy was usually fouled by oil slicks. His only aid to aiming the torpedo was a graduated scale engraved on the inside of the canopy and an aiming spike in front of him.

Left, bottom: A *Neger* abandoned on the beach at Anzio in April 1944, the pilot having suffocated – a not uncommon occurrence. *Neger*s were first used on the night of 20/21 April 1944 and sustained some 80 per cent mortality. Despite German claims as to their successes, post-war evaluation shows that they were responsible for sinking three minesweepers and a destroyer, plus damage to a cruiser and a destroyer. A development of the *Neger* was the *Marder* (Pine), which had the added advantage of being able to dive to 30m but proved no more successful in action, sinking one destroyer, one LCT and a balloon ship.

Right, top: The next German weapon was the *Molch* (Salamander), which was an electrically driven one-man torpedo carrier. Two G7e torpedoes were slung one on each side of the craft and the operator sat in a small conning tower at the stern. Ease of production was of prime importance in the *Molch*'s design and so the craft used as many standard torpedo components as possible.

Right, centre: A *Molch* in warpaint being towed ashore at the German Navy's torpedo trials establishment at Eckenforde in the summer of 1944. A total of 393 *Molch*es were built and employed off Anzio and the Netherlands but to little effect: the *Molch* was complicated to operate and the crews lacked proper training or support.

Right, bottom: The *Biber* (Beaver) was a more sophisticated craft powered by a petrol motor when on the surface (never an ideal form of propulsion for a submarine) and an electric motor when submerged. The armament consisted of the usual two G7e torpedoes carried in recesses in the pressure hull. This craft was fitted with a proper periscope, which is here shown camouflaged with a 'nest' to disguise the tell-tale 'feather'.

Above, left: The operator's position inside a *Biber*, showing the austere nature of the design. The control wheel is in the centre, with the rudder indicator at lower left and the hydroplane indicator at lower right. Above, from left to right, are the gauges for engine oil pressure, oxygen pressure, battery voltage and LP and HP air. The three armoured glass ports are visible, but the operator was also given a fixed, forward-facing periscope.

Above, right: *Biber*s were first employed off the Normandy beaches on the night of 29 August 1944. They carried out only one operation before their base at Fécamp was overrun and the *Biber*s were abandoned on the beach as seen here. They moved to the Netherlands and began operations from the Scheldt estuary on 23 December 1944, but the latter were suspended after more than fifty craft had been lost.
Below: The Soviet battleship

Arkhangelsk, the target for Operation 'Caesar' which was a raid by six *Biber*s on the Soviet anchorage at Murmansk in January 1945. Three U-boats (*U295*, *U318* and *U716*) were specially modified to carry two *Biber*s but the operation was dogged by mishaps despite intensive training by the submarines and *Biber* operators. All six craft were declared unserviceable en route to the objective and the operation was abandoned.

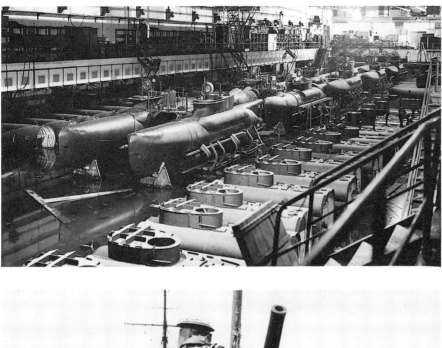

Left, top: *Biber* was followed by the Type XXVIIB U-boat, better known as the *Seehund*, shown here in series production at DWK's Kiel factory. Armed with two torpedoes, *Seehund* carried a crew of two and had considerable qualities of endurance. The *Seehund*s came into service too late to do any damage but they posed a significant threat none the less. They were too small to give an asdic return and were all but inaudible to the hydrophones of the day.

Left, centre: Explosive motor boats – fast motor boats packed with high explosives, which were pointed at the target – were another special weapon favoured by Italy, Germany and Japan. This photograph shows the wrecked British cruiser *York* at Suda Bay in Crete following a successful Italian motor boat attack on the night of 25 March 1941. Subsequent Italian operations were not so successful – in an attack on Malta three months later all nine motor boats were sunk, the defenders having radar which robbed the attackers of the precious advantage of surprise.

Left, bottom: The Germans and Japanese also experimented with explosive motor boats. This photograph shows a Japanese *Shinyo* craft being put through its paces after being captured during the Okinawa Campaign. Unlike the Germans and Italians, however, the Japanese did not provide the operators with a means of abandoning their craft before hitting the target. The operator rode his craft to an apocalyptic end.

10. LIFE AT SEA

Warfare has been defined as long periods of inaction followed by brief moments of frantic activity. The same is true of naval warfare, but the sea is a constant companion and hazard – and no respecter of nationalities.

Left, upper: Rough weather, as shown here in the Arctic in February 1945, was a constant companion to life at sea. It brought its own strains and dangers which piled on top of those caused by the threat of enemy action.

Below, left: *Kapitän zur See* Karl Topp on the bridge of *Tirpitz* in northern waters in the spring of 1942. Note the superb winter clothing supplied to officers and ratings alike.

Below, right: The ice-encrusted bridge of a Canadian corvette in the North Atlantic. The build-up of ice was potentially dangerous because it interfered with a ship's stability.

Above: The only solution to the problem of ice was to remove it – by hand. Here sailors on the cruiser HMS *Scylla* clear the forecastle of snow and ice in the spring of 1943.
Below, left: The lookout on a German warship in Norwegian waters. Even in 'friendly' waters a constant lookout had to be maintained. Again, note the superb quality of the foul-weather clothing.
Below, right: There could be few more miserable duties than those of a lookout in bad weather, as exemplified by these two Polish seamen aboard the destroyer ORP *Piorun*.

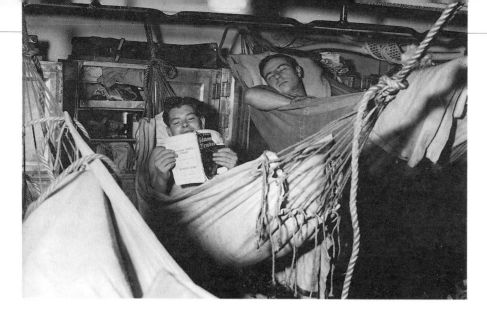

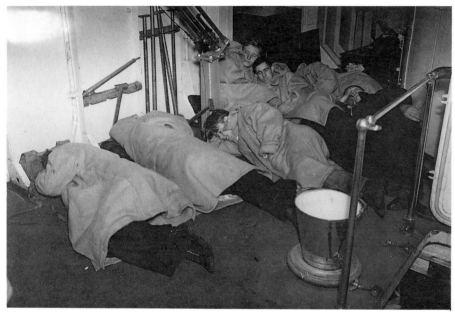

British destroyer HMS *Glow-worm* wait their turn to go aboard the German cruiser *Admiral Hipper* (see Chapter 1 for the circumstances of *Glow-worm*'s loss).

Far left, bottom: The look on the face of this German U-boat survivor expresses his gratitude at being picked up by HMCS *Swansea* in 1944.

Middle left, top: A 6in gun crew closed up in their turret aboard the British cruiser HMS *Sheffield* in the winter of 1941–42. In areas where there the risk of action was high, ships' companies had to remain at a state of readiness.

Middle left, centre: These three seamen were fortunate: picked up after eighty-three days on the raft. Two of their companions died and were buried at sea.

Middle left, bottom: HMS *Sheffield* buries her dead after the *Bismarck* action in May 1941. A total of over 150,000 personnel were killed at sea in all navies – most would have been accorded the traditional burial at sea.

Left, upper: The hammock – traditional method of sleeping at sea since time immemorial. This photograph was taken aboard the British aircraft carrier HMS *Formidable* in 1945.

Left, lower: Ratings sleeping on deck in the destroyer HMS *Jackal* in 1940. For operational reasons it was not always possible to sling hammocks. In these circumstances men slept on the deck as best they could.

Far left, top: Another miserable lookout, this time on the French corvette *Aconit*. In small ships at sea in winter, with primitive cooking facilities, life quickly degenerated into a miserable round of cold food, wet clothes and little sleep.

Far left, centre: Traditionally, a sailor whose ship has been sunk becomes a mariner in distress rather than an enemy. All belligerents – except the Japanese – rescued survivors if it were practicable, although sometimes it was not possible to do so for operational reasons. Here oil-soaked men from the

Top, left: Troops on passage to the various overseas theatres endured even greater discomforts as seen in this photograph.

Above, left: The warm climate of the Far East ensured that it was possible to sleep outside, as these aircrew are doing in a British escort carrier of the Eastern Fleet in 1945.

Top, right: The fore-ends of the British submarine HMS *Storm* on her return from the Far East in 1945. Submariners endured greater discomforts than other sailors in terms of overcrowding and lack of facilities. However, their *esprit de corps* and the plentiful facilities of depot ships more than compensated for this.

Above, right: Deep below the waterline in all ships of all navies worked the men of the engine and boiler rooms. This photograph shows the boiler room of the British destroyer HMS *Tartar* in the Far East in 1945. In tropical climates heat exhaustion in the machinery spaces was a problem, particularly in British ships.

Right: Officers and enlisted men gather on the fantail of an American cruiser in the Pacific for Divine Service.

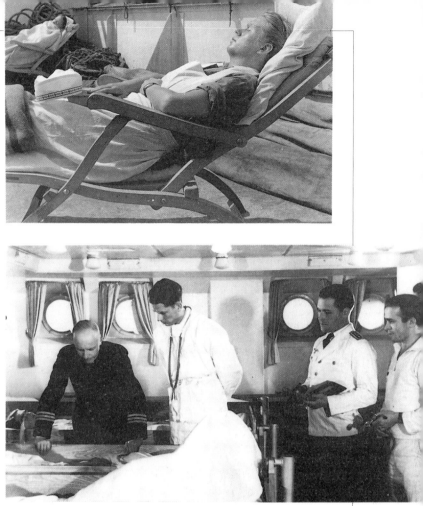

Above, left: A casualty is transferred from an American destroyer to a larger vessel where more sophisticated medical facilities would be available.

Top, right: A German nurse takes some time off from her duties in the Mediterranean. Hospital ships were protected by international law. Although there were a few regrettable exceptions, this convention was honoured by all sides – including the Japanese.

Above, right: Capital ships had quite extensive medical facilities. Here the medical officer in *Tirpitz* conducts his morning ward round.

Right: A Chief Petty Officer Cook samples the day's offering aboard *Tirpitz*.

Right, upper: Potato-peeling. The ratings are British but the photograph could have been taken anywhere.

Right, lower: The chef in a British escort carrier. British food was monotonous, but so long as the British sailor had his large roast dinner followed by an indigestible sponge pudding (in any climate) he was quite content.

Below, left: The manpower needs of all the navies were immense. Training programmes had to be condensed as much as possible in order to get men to sea. Here British trainees study models of ships in the fleet at HMS *Raleigh* in Devon.

Below, right: US sailors learn the traditional art of rowing.

Middle right, top: French sailors learn the equally traditional art of tying knots.

Middle right, centre: British sailors at elementary gun drill. The demands of war did not prevent gunnery being treated as a quasi-religion within the Royal Navy.

Middle right, bottom: US midshipmen at Annapolis get their taste of shiphandling on a YP craft in Chesapeake Bay.

Below right: Japanese sailors salute their parents on completion of basic training.
Bottom right: German U-boat men return from patrol and are greeted by their flotilla staff and female auxiliaries from the base. All sailors, of whatever navy, hoped for a safe return to land.

11. VICTORY AND DEFEAT

Winning or losing is an inevitable consequence of warfare. Britain and America suffered temporary reverses but were spared the humiliation of total capitulation which was the fate of the French, Italians, Germans and Japanese. After nearly five years of total war, the various surrenders were accomplished with a style and dignity reminiscent of an earlier age. After the surrenders the victors had to turn their hands to a host of new tasks such as reconstruction and repatriation of PoWs. The end of hostilities created a host of new difficulties which had to be faced as the various navies slimmed down and faced a new world order.

Below: The French Navy was the first to experience defeat following the armistice at Compiègne on 21 June. Although the Germans indicated that they did not want to take over the French fleet, the British were worried that the ships might fall into German hands. The British gave French squadrons based in ports outside France the choice of joining the British, disarmament and subsequent internment in the Caribbean, or being sunk *in situ*. This photograph shows the cruiser *Duquesne* and destroyer *Le Fortun* interned at Alexandria where the French Admiral Godfoy opted for internment.

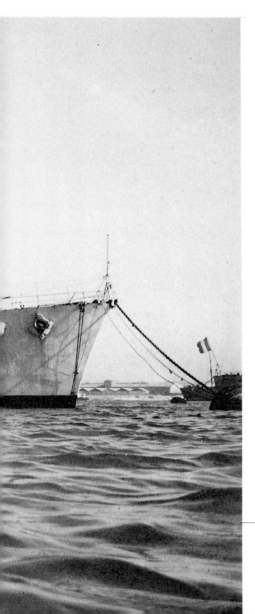

Top: At Oran, however, things did not go so smoothly and on 3 July 1940, after negotiations had broken down, the British opened fire. The battleships *Provence*, *Dunkerque* and *Bretagne* were sunk or disabled and more than 1,200 French seamen were killed. It was a bitter end to the Anglo-French alliance. In Britain too, French ships were seized and their crews imprisoned. They had the option of joining the Free French forces being established under General Charles de Gaulle or being repatriated to France. It was a cruel dilemma.

Above: The French fleet lingered in an ambiguous state until 1942 when, following the Allied landings in North Africa and the subsequent dissolution of the Vichy regime, the French authorities ordered the ships at Toulon to be scuttled.

Left, upper: The Italian battleship *Vittorio Veneto* with the cruiser *Emmanuele Filiberto Duca d'Aosta* sailing for Malta on 8 September 1943 for internment. Italy had concluded an armistice with the Allies on 3 September following the fall of Mussolini's government. A condition of the armistice was that the Italian fleet surrender at Malta. The surrender did not proceed without incident: the battleship *Roma* (ex-*Littorio*) was sunk en route by a German radio-controlled glider bomb on 9 September.

Left, lower: 'Be pleased to inform their Lordships that the Italian fleet now lies beneath the guns of the fortress of Malta' was the signal sent to London by Admiral Sir Andrew Cunningham. The surrender was a fitting end to the siege of Malta throughout which the inhabitants and garrison had endured considerable privations. Ships visible in the photograph are (bottom to top) the cruiser *Eugenio di Savoia*, the battleship *Caio Duilio* and the battleship *Andrea Doria*.

Right, top: Admiral Dinsioni Oliva, Commander-in-Chief of the Italian fleet, comes ashore at Malta to be greeted by Cunningham's Chief of Staff, Commodore Royer Dick.

Right, centre: Oliva in discussions with Cunningham concerning the disposition of his fleet. At Malta the ships were inspected, disarmed and then sent to internment in the Great Bitter Lakes.

Right, bottom: A trot of Italian submarines laid up at Malta. Some of these craft would eventually see service in a training role on the Allied side when Italy became a co-belligerent.

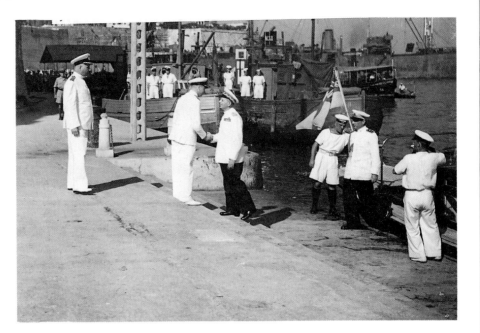

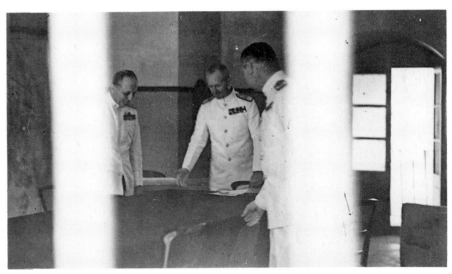

Far left, upper: The Italian surrender was, largely, an amicable affair. Here British and Italian sailors 'spin some dits' at Taranto following the British landing there on 9 September; soon some of these Italian sailors would be fighting on the Allied side.

Far left, lower: The Italian naval headquarters at Taranto 'under new management' as the headquarters for a British Rear-Admiral whose flag flies on the flagstaff.

Below: Two Italian sail training ships looking very forlorn, laid up at Brindisi: *Amerigo Vespucci* (left) and *Cristoforo Colombo*.

Colombo was eventually ceded to the USSR but *Vespucci* remains in Italian service to this day.

Left: When Germany capitulated on 7 May 1945 with the signing of the surrender at Rheims, all U-boats at sea were ordered to cease operations. Subsequently they were ordered to make their way on the surface and flying a large black flag to pre-arranged assembly points. This photograph shows some of a group of fifteen U-boats heading for Loch Eriboll on the west coast of Scotland.

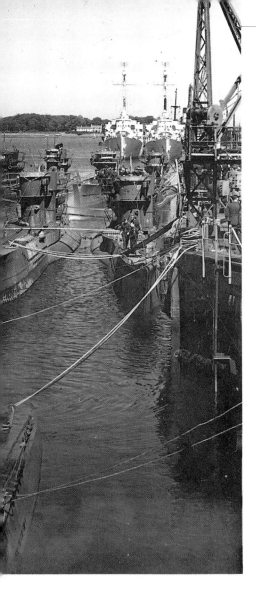

Far left, top: *U1305*, a Type VIIC U-boat, seen from a motor launch at Loch Eriboll. The black surrender flag is just visible flying from the periscope. The Germans may have surrendered but the gunner on the 20mm mounting in the foreground is not taking any chances.

Far left, centre: Once at the collection points, the U-boats were disarmed and their crews dispatched to PoW camps to await repatriation, apart from a small number of personnel kept aboard for essential maintenance. Here a seaman in *U826* at Loch Eriboll prepares to dump the torpedo director over the side.

Far left, bottom: Another gaggle of U-boats heading for surrender at Scapa Flow under the watchful eye of HMS *Launceston Castle*.

Left, upper: U-boats laid up at Lisahally in Northern Ireland, one of the specified collection points for German submarines. Back row (left to right): *U2326, U1105, U826, U802, U293.* Middle row (left to right): *U1009, U1059, U1305, U1109.* Front row: the outboard boat (stern only) is *U516* but the Type VII boat inboard is unknown. These boats were all subsequently sunk in Operation 'Deadlight'.

Left, lower: *U2326*, a Type XXIII submarine designed for operations in coastal waters, secured alongside at Dundee. The Type XXIIIs were not deployed in sufficient numbers to have any effect on hostilities but this particular boat was actively sinking ships in the Firth of Forth as late as May 1945.

Below: Admiral Sir Max Horton, Commander-in-Chief Western Approaches, goes down the brow to *U532* in the Gladstone Dock at Liverpool after the surrender. *U532* was a Type IX and had just entered European waters after a hazardous voyage from Japan carrying strategic materials when the surrender was announced. Among those saluting Horton is *Fregattenkapitän* Ottoheinrich Junker, the submarine's commanding officer.

Right: A trot of Type VII U-boats secured at Wilhelmshaven awaiting orders from the British authorities. They are the lucky ones: out of a force of 39,000, 28,000 U-boat crewmen were killed and 5,000 taken prisoner – a casualty rate of 85 per cent, the highest sustained by any service of any belligerent.

Below: Triumph over the U-boats. *U776* arrives at Westminster to be opened to the public.

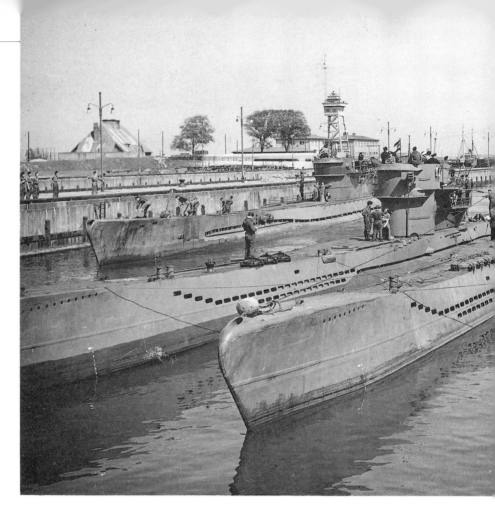

Below: Crowds along the quayside at Copenhagen following the Royal Navy's entry into the city in May 1945. Shown here are the cruisers *Birmingham* and Dido (moored further up the quay) with the destroyer *Zodiac* between them. Outboard of Dido is the destroyer *Zest* and further up the quay from *Dido* lie the destroyers *Zephyr* and *Zealous*. **Above:** A Royal Marine sentry from HMS *Birmingham* enjoys the limelight. The reception given to the British by the Danes was overwhelming.

Right, top: German delegates attending a meeting in HMS *Dido* to discuss minesweeping and other matters are shown over the side by an armed sentry with none of the usual courtesies accorded officers of a foreign navy.

Right, centre: *Schnellboote* arrive at HMS *Hornet*, the coastal forces' base at Gosport, to surrender in May 1945. The two officers on the bridge have turned their backs on the photographer.

Right, bottom: When Royal Navy parties reached Germany they found a scene of total devastation. This is Kiel with the wreck of the pocket battleship *Admiral Scheer*, bombed on 9 April 1945, in the background and the bow sections of two uncompleted Type XXI U-boats in the foreground. Note the devastation in the dock area behind.

Right, top: *Schnellboote* personnel embarked in a British RML at Felixstowe for the first of many journeys to a PoW camp. For them the war was over.

Right, centre: The wrecked cruiser *Köln* at Wilhelmshaven with some of her crew, or dock workers, enjoying an alfresco meal on the upper deck.

Right, bottom: Torpedoes abandoned on the quayside at Kiel. The huge amount of ordnance littering Germany posed considerable problems with regard to its disposal.

Above: The personnel problems caused by the surrender were immense. Here German officers and men register at Kiel for denazification procedures.

Above centre: Two German destroyers, flying the White Ensign, arrive at Kiel with German personnel evacuated from Norway. The British had to use German ships and personnel for a number of tasks, including repatriation duties and minesweeping, for some time after the surrender.

Right upper: The fruits of victory: British personnel at Kiel with some liberated German bullion.

Right lower: German merchant shipping gathered at Methil. Any surviving German merchant ships were seized and brought to Britain for distribution to those companies who had suffered losses during the war. However, such an exchange could not hope to match the vast number of Allied merchant ships sunk in the Atlantic.

Left: After defeat came reconstruction. The bomb-blasted harbours of northern German had to be cleared for British use and for the resumption of normal activity. Here a scuttled Type XXI U-boat is lifted clear of a jetty at Kiel.

Above right: The summer of 1945 was a time for victory parades. Here the Royal Marines exercise the traditional rights of a conqueror by marching through Hamburg on 4 July 1945 with a band playing followed by a Naval guard with fixed bayonets. Whether the Germans appreciated the symbolism is not clear but the event certainly drew a crowd.

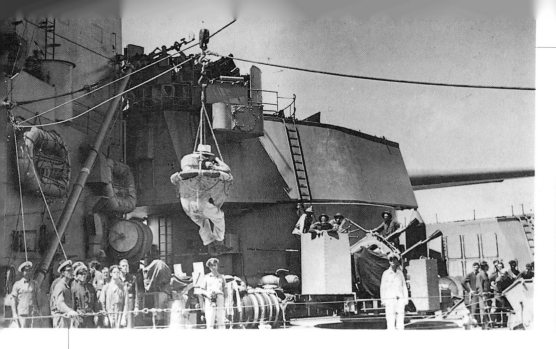

Above, left: On to the Far East, where on 14 August the Japanese agreed to surrender unconditionally. Military forces moved swiftly to occupy Japan. A small British task force joined the American Third Fleet and entered Tokyo Bay on 27 August. Here the Japanese pilot is brought aboard the British flagship HMS *Duke of York* by jackstay transfer. It turned out that the pilot was incompetent and his 'interpreter' spoke no English. Their services were dispensed with.

Above, centre: The Japanese battleship *Nagato* in Tokyo Bay. She was the sole surviving capital ship of a fleet which had dominated the Pacific and East Indies in the early part of the war. She was subsequently expended in atomic tests at Bikini Atoll.

Right, upper: The final act of the Second World War took place aboard the American battleship *Missouri* on 2 September 1945 when representatives of the Japanese government and high command signed the surrender document. Here representatives of the various Allied powers line up to await the arrival of the Japanese delegation. From left to right:

General Hsu Yung-Chang (China); Admiral Sir Bruce Fraser (Great Britain); Lieutenant-General K. Derevyanko (USSR); General Sir Thomas Blamey (Australia); Colonel L. Moore-Gosgrove (Canada) and General Jacques Leclerc (France).

Right, lower: General of the Army Douglas MacArthur signs the surrender for the Allied Powers. Behind him stand Generals Wainwright and Percival, both looking thin after their Japanese captivity, who had surrendered to the Japanese in 1942 in the Philippines and Singapore respectively. For them this must have been a sweet moment. MacArthur brought an end to the ceremony with the words, 'These proceedings are closed'.

Far right, upper: All over the Pacific and South-East Asia the Japanese were surrendering. Here their delegation leaves the municipal buildings at Singapore after the surrender ceremony there on 12 September.

Far right, lower: The flags of the Allied Powers fly from the mainmast of the British flagship HMS *Duke of York* in the evening of 2 September.

Left, upper: British officers inspect the mangled stern of the Japanese cruiser *Myoko* at Singapore.

Left: An impassive Vice-Admiral Ruitaka Fujita arrives for the surrender ceremony at Hong Kong on 16 September. British observers were amused to note that among the admiral's decorations were the

British 1914–18 War Medal and the 1918 Victory Medal.

Above, centre: Surrender or not, the Allies were taking no chances with the Japanese. Here men from the British destroyers *Whirlwind* and *Quadrant* watch Japanese personnel at a Shinyo boat base on Picnic Island near Hong Kong. In the end most Japanese obeyed the orders of their high command and there was no mass resistance.

Above, right: The war was over but there was much to be done. This is the hangar of the aircraft carrier *Colossus*, configured as a hospital ward for released Allied prisoners of war. With the coming of peace the role of the victorious navies changed to that of relief and reconstruction.

Below: The escort carrier HMS *Speaker* leaves Tokyo Bay on 3 September 1945 carrying the first PoWs to return to the UK. As the ship moved slowly through the crowded anchorage, every rail was lined with cheering sailors giving the ex-PoWs an emotional send-off.

With the peace came retrenchment. Navies slimmed down during the post-war period as resources were channelled towards welfare and reconstruction. Here the British battlecruiser HMS *Renown*, veteran of Force H in the Mediterranean, pays off at Devonport on 2 June 1948. For old ships as well as the officers and men of the various navies, the war was over.